YOUR
SECRETS

KEVIN MCKEOWN WITH DAVE STERN

ARE MY
BUSINESS

A Security Expert Reveals How
Your Trash, License Plate, Credit
Cards, Computer, and Even Your
Mail Make You an Easy Target for
Today's Information Thieves

LONGSTREET
Atlanta, Georgia

Published by
LONGSTREET, INC.
A subsidiary of Cox Newspapers
A subsidiary of Cox Enterprises, Inc.
2140 Newmarket Parkway
Suite 122
Marietta, GA 30067
www.lspress.com

Printed in the United States of America

1st printing 1999

Library of Congress Catalog Card Number: 99-61754

ISBN: 1-56352-577-1

Jacket and book design by Megan Wilson

ACKNOWLEDGMENTS

Heartfelt appreciation goes to the people who made this book happen.
Thanks to:

Lisa Bankoff, ICM agent and miracle worker. Lisa's guidance and
valued leadership through the entire process ensured an enjoyable,
successful journey. And ICM's Patrick Price for his tireless input and
exacting assistance.

Sherry Wade, editor at Longstreet Press, and this book's mentor,
leader, and savior. Her keen eye, brilliant mind, and treasured direction made this book what it is. It was an honor to work for, and
learn from, Sherry.

Chuck Perry, Longstreet president and editor, and Steve Gracie,
Longstreet general manager, for authorizing this book and generous-
ly giving their time and talents—in Atlanta and Los Angeles—to offer
insight, share experiences, and provide forceful encouragement.

Chuck and Steve also lead a group of great minds at Longstreet, some of
whom need special mention.
Thanks to:

Megan Wilson (book and cover design): A true artist!
Amy Burton (publicity manager) and Beth Dickey (publicist):
Fearless and determined!
Scott Bard (director of marketing and sales administration) for his
unselfish knowledge of book marketing.
Thomas Cogburn, Tammy Eigel, and Robyn Richardson for their
help and friendship in L.A.
Katherine Wages for her always friendly and helpful administrative
assistance.

And special thanks to:
Suzanne De Galan, former senior editor at Longstreet, for her confi-
dence in the original proposal that made this work a Longstreet book.

Direct all the praise to the people above—
everything else to the appreciative authors.

The newly paranoid co-author wishes to thank several additional people . . .
you know who you are.

TABLE OF CONTENTS

TABLE OF CONTENTS (CONT.)

YOUR
SECRETS

KEVIN MCKEOWN WITH DAVE STERN

ARE MY
BUSINESS

INTRODUCTION

THE MUSTARD MAN AND ME

Having your car towed is never a pleasant experience. But having your car towed in New York City is a special kind of treat, one you would only wish on your worst enemy.

It was more than ten years ago. It was the fourth time I discovered either an empty space or another vehicle parked where my car once was. Was it stolen? Was it towed? At the time, there was no centralized telephone number to see if anyone other than a thief had your car. It could have been anywhere, taken by the sheriff's office, the city marshal's, the New York City Department of Transportation — whichever agency got to it first.

So you start with the cops — they don't know where your car is, and they definitely don't care. The sheriff's office doesn't have your car on their overnight pickup list, but that doesn't mean they definitely don't have it. Whomever you talk to, they'll tell you the same thing: "You have to go down to the tow pound and check."

Now, depending on where you get towed — East Side, West

Side, downtown, uptown — the "City" tow trucks can take your car to any one of a few different tow pounds. All of them are inconveniently located. My favorite is the tow pound on the Hudson River near Thirty-fourth Street. You actually have to sprint across the equivalent of an eight-lane highway to get there. And once inside, you get to stand in a long, slow-moving line.

You can always tell the virgin towee: full of righteous anger — "the sign wasn't clearly marked," "they towed me before the space was illegal" — ready to fight for justice. This Saturday morning, one happens to be standing right in front of me. A well-dressed gentleman, fuming, barely able to contain himself. He looks like the type of guy who would start off threatening to write the mayor and be screaming obscenities as he walked out the door.

"Next," the clerk grunts.

I settle back to watch as the show begins.

First off, this guy is utterly shocked, and a little insulted, that the clerk won't take his personal check.

"Cash . . . cash only . . . cash only. Can't you read?" the clerk asks.

Of course this guy can read. He announces that he's the head-master of XYZ prep school outside of Philadelphia. "I've never bounced a check in my life," he says. I suddenly realize this guy reminds me of the man in the back of the Rolls Royce in the Grey Poupon commercial.

The clerk turns to her counterpart, mimicking what the man just said. Both clerks start to laugh.

The headmaster's face falls, as he begins to understand that there will be no Grey Poupon served at this New York City tow pound.

I don't know what came over me. I wasn't working, my guard was down, I guess. He seemed nice enough. I walk up next to him at the window. "Hey, I'll help you out. I have some extra cash on me."

The gentleman smiles, "Why, that's most kind of you. I'll drive right to the bank and pay you back immediately."

Now the clerks start laughing at both of us.

Ignoring them, I follow the headmaster gentleman (let's call him the Mustard Man) to an ATM at Forty-second Street and Sixth Avenue. I watch his car while he dashes into the bank. We don't want him to get towed away again, not before he pays me back, anyway. He returns and counts the cash out into my hand. He's genuinely appreciative. For a moment, it seems as if he's going to hug me. And I'm equally glad I was able to help him.

"You're very nice, very trusting," he says. Then he smiles. "You're not from New York, are you?"

I smile right back at him. "I am. Born in the Bronx. And I guess I am a trusting person. But since I know your full name, your wife's name, your address, date of birth, the name of your bank, your license plate number, the name of your insurance company, and the name of the school where you're the head-master . . ."

At this point, Mustard Man's jaw practically hits the floor.

". . . if you decided not to pay me back, I didn't think I'd have trouble finding you."

He swallows and smiles guardedly, eyeing me like I've become some kind of lunatic. All of a sudden, he's in a rush to get away. With a last, hurried thank you, he hops into his car and drives off.

I was just trying to be nice, I swear. I can understand Mustard Man being a bit alarmed at the realization that I knew so much about him. I wouldn't have liked it either. Standing in line behind him, my natural curiosity got the better of me. I peeked.

I got his wife's name, the name of his bank, and his account number from his checkbook.

His date of birth, full name, and address from his driver's license.

His insurance company and place of business from his insur-ance card.

Now bear in mind, I really didn't care about this guy. But imagine if I did?

Imagine if the Mustard Man were you, and I'd gotten into line behind you at the tow pound because your wife/hus-band/boss/coworker/competitor/old enemy hired me to find out everything I could about you. Or I saw the expensive clothes you were wearing, and I knew that meant you had money. And I wanted some. All the information I mentioned above would have been duly entered in my hand-held electronic organizer (it would have looked like I was playing a computer game).

Even if you had been more careful than the Mustard Man in guarding your information from my view, even if all I had to go on was your name or your license plate number, I could have found you. More to the point, I could have found out any number of things about you.

You can't imagine how many databases your address is sitting in.

You don't know how easy it is to find out how much you make for a living.

What credit cards you use.

Whom you call on the telephone.

You — and the vast majority of records containing valuable information about you — are incredibly vulnerable. For the last twenty years, my job has been to exploit that vulnerability.

Frankly, I've had a lot of fun doing it.

I've gone from sleeping in dumpsters to spending the night in thousand-dollar hotel rooms, from masquerading as a corporate mailboy to running million-dollar corporate board meetings. I've combed through dusty archives in small-town city halls and mainframe computers in major metropolises, used quirks in the law and legal, but very unorthodox, investigative methods. Whether I was working for Goldman Sachs or Prudential Life, a local sheriff or the federal government, Robert De Niro or a friend in need, I've been able — through patience, perseverance, and what I like to call "creative luck" — to get results.

Over the last two decades, I've watched the information-gathering industry grow into a multibillion-dollar concern, one that gets bigger every year.

And although the information-gathering business has always been a little bit out of control, even I'm alarmed now. The collection, use, and disbursement of all kinds of data are now at a reckless, dangerous level.

I, like you, have peeked at and have been peeked upon by the Mustard Men and Women of the world. Our innate curiosity and thirst for knowledge is a double-edged sword. Information — knowledge — is indeed power. But that power can be abused at any level. It's important never to underestimate the driving force behind the search for information, be it the toddler, driven to find the means to reach the cookie jar, or a seemingly "regular" person determined to find, exploit, abuse, or market information regarding you.

I've been driven to uncover information by many factors: superiors' orders, money, and a simple, undefined desire. I confess, it's not a good feeling being the target of a search. We are more vulnerable than ever since technology started propelling information at unfamiliar speeds. The time has come to refocus the many facets of the information business.

Thanks to computerized recordkeeping, dozens of companies now have your social security number, your phone number, your date of birth (at some point in the past, you've no doubt given it away, either on the Internet, over the phone, or in a credit application).

In the old days, somebody who wanted to get the dirt on you — an angry customer, your ex-husband, an old business partner — would turn to a traditional private eye, a gumshoe, to dig it up. Today, that information sits in a database, waiting to be discovered. There's a growing army of people out there capable of making those discoveries.

And that army isn't sitting around, waiting for business to come knocking on its door.

In the most frightening development of all, these new information warriors seek out the dirt first — and then find customers for it, such as television shows, tabloid newspapers, special prosecutors. In today's rumor-mongering, celebrity-driven culture, "private" information is an alien concept.

I remember being at a fund-raiser organized to help defray legal expenses incurred by senior CIA agent Clair George. Looking around the room, I realized that every single person there was a government-trained information-gathering expert — who had since moved on into the enormously lucrative private sector. Their focus was no longer on the common good as much as it was on the bottom line — and on your personal, "private" records.

You need to be aware of how those prying eyes work, and you need protection against them.

This book will give you both.

I'm going to show you what to do when you're on your telephone, when you're driving in your car, when you leave your home. I'll tell you what you need to teach your children and your elderly relatives so that they can protect themselves. I'll tell you some stories about the methods I've used to get dirt on the bad guys — and the dirty tricks the most experienced con artists use to get at what's important to you. And I'll give you a chance to see how effective some of these methods are by helping you "play detective" yourself.

Every chapter in this book ends with a list of practical tips. The odds are good that you, or someone close to you, will have use for them, sooner than you think.

Many of those tips deal with the high-tech threats mentioned above; many of them are common-sense defenses against more traditional thievery. As important as those tips are, my focus will be on the mind-set that makes you vulnerable. Change that, and you, your loved ones, and your valuable assets will be safer — no matter what technological advances the future brings.

And before we begin:

The laws covering your right to privacy — and access to your information — are in a state of flux. Keep current on what's legal, and what isn't, by utilizing the resources we list in the back of this book.

A final word about the stories in the book. Every one of them is true. We have changed some of the names (and identifying background details) to protect the innocent . . . and to make less work for the lawyers.

Kevin McKeown, Washington, D.C., July 19, 1999

1

YOUR HABITS

THIS LOOKS LIKE A JOB FOR SUPERMAN

His address was useless.

His employer hadn't seen him in weeks.

He'd made no contact with friends, relatives, or business associates since the day he disappeared.

Even his mother hadn't heard from him.

My job: Track this missing man down and, in the process, recover the quarter-million dollars he'd ripped off from one of America's largest banks.

It seemed like I might need super-hearing, or X-ray vision. But all I had were the facts of the case as Citibank presented them to me.

Much to their embarrassment, the bank had approved a $250,000 loan to this gentleman, who'd presented his apartment as collateral. The only problem was, this guy was a tenant. He didn't actually own the apartment. He'd picked a time when the owner was out of town to hit up the bank for the loan.

By the time my team of investigators and I arrived on the

scene, the con man had disappeared off the face of the earth. He couldn't be found anywhere. We checked his place of business and conducted a series of interviews with his neighbors, acquaintances, and relatives.

All we managed to find out was that he spent a lot of time down in Florida, and that he was an avid comic book collector. His favorite comic: the Justice League of America — a team of superheroes that included Batman, Wonder Woman, and the Man of Steel — Superman himself.

I did a little research and discovered that the first time this group of heroes teamed up was in a comic book called *The Brave and the Bold*, issue #28, originally published in February 1960. According to the *Official Overstreet Comic Book Price Guide* (the comic book collector's bible), a copy of *The Brave and the Bold #28* in excellent condition was, at the time, worth close to two thousand dollars.

How badly, I wondered, would our friend want that particular comic book? We thought it worth our while — and our client's money — to find out.

We ran an ad in every possible publication in southern Florida, advertising *two* copies of *The Brave and The Bold #28*, in excellent condition, for sale at $650 each. The ad ran for five months. We got two dozen or so legitimate inquiries to our ad. All of the callers offered to pay more than we were asking — we could have made some decent money had we actually had the comics!

Finally, our friend called and left a message: He, too, was very interested in the comics we had to offer. (How did we know it was the missing man? We played the answering machine tape back for the people in New York who knew his voice.) We quickly made arrangements to meet at his apartment and finalize the deal.

A few days later, his doorbell rang. But when he answered it, instead of his long-sought-after comic, he found two Dade County detectives, who promptly took him into custody, pending his transfer to New York, where he was going to stand trial for bank fraud.

At his trial, we discovered the reason this guy had been so hard to track down was because he'd "borrowed" the identity of a young relative who had been killed in an automobile accident. We would have been waiting a long time for this guy to surface under his own name.

Normal investigative procedures would never have been successful against our quarry. We had to use what we knew of his desires against him.

Investigators are hungry for this kind of knowledge. It helps them identify and track down their targets. It can also help establish the kind of common bond that causes even the most careful person to lower his guard.

And in that instant, he's vulnerable.

Think of this type of information as your "behavioral fingerprints." You leave them everywhere. Those itty-bitty things you need, like to have, or enjoy doing. If you're a businessman it may be the types of journals you read, the clubs and organizations you belong to, those brand-name items you just can't live without. Expensive suits and shoes, mannerisms, and hobbies can sometimes be more useful in tracking a person down than a picture.

Even better, unlike a person's appearance, which changes over time — or can be altered with a ten-dollar bottle of hair color — a list of your behavioral fingerprints will identify you twenty years from now as surely as it will today.

What, you may ask, do your behavioral fingerprints have to do with the assault on your privacy we're talking about?

Today, more and more of those fingerprints — the things you like to buy, the places you like to shop, the people you like to call — are being systematically analyzed, broken down into discrete bits of data, and entered into computers. Your consumer profile is valuable information to any one of a thousand firms out there . . . particularly when it's cross-referenced against your medical records, your employment history, who you interact with, and your banking records.

The trained individual can easily access the information in those databases. And if the information can't be readily accessed, it can usually be quickly and inexpensively purchased.

A few years ago I made a very simple mistake. I ordered a subscription to the *Wall Street Journal*, and had it delivered — in my name — to the waterfront location where I was staying for a few months. I wanted to be able to roll out of bed and hit the beach: I didn't even want to walk to the store for the daily newspaper.

I should have made the effort.

Junk mail addressed to me — junk mail offering the kinds of products and services that the affluent, college-educated typical reader of the *Wall Street Journal* would have been interested in — started arriving within two weeks.

I immediately canceled the subscription and shot a letter of protest to the publisher. But though he tried, even he — the head honcho — couldn't stop my name and address from spreading like wildfire across those databases. I'm sure mail is still being delivered to that address with my name on it.

THE FREQUENT LIARS CLUB

A friend of mine had been hired by Prudential Insurance to investigate a female attorney who was receiving a $6,500 monthly disability payment . . . tax-free. This thirty-nine-year-old woman claimed she had developed such a severe case of carpal tunnel syndrome that she was unable to walk, sit, stand, or read for any lengthy period of time without feeling intense pain. The report of her pain would bring tears to your eyes.

The woman lived on Manhattan's Upper West Side in a small apartment building. Prudential's investigators had been watching the address for months and had failed to catch sight of her. My friend had also done extensive surveillance and come up empty. But her bills were getting paid on time. Someone was taking care of her cat. And *somebody* was depositing that $6,500 check every month.

Where was she?

We did a little discrete investigating of her friends and former coworkers. It turned out this woman came from a respectable family background, was well educated, and she lived (at least ostensibly) in the most cultured city in the United States.

It seemed reasonable to assume that she traveled a lot.

A person who travels a lot is, by definition, a frequent flyer. Airlines keep computer databases of their frequent-flyer patrons. I found out that she was a member of several frequent-flyer programs: TWA, American, and United. But the trail dead-ended there: We found no significant recent activity on any of the airlines she used.

I was frustrated. My friend was frustrated. Prudential was frustrated.

A year passed.

I was working another case that took me a block away from this woman's apartment. We (I had two women working with me on a fraud case) ended work early in the afternoon.

Noticing where we were, I decided to call my friend.

"Anything ever happen on that Prudential insurance fraud case?" I asked him. He told me it was still an open investigation, that no progress had been made over the last year. We agreed I should give it one more try.

I had the girls go up and ring the attorney's doorbell. I sat on a bench across the street, in front of a schoolyard.

Initially, there was no response. But as the girls were walking down the steps, away from the apartment, a man came rushing out after them.

"Are you looking for Sandy?" he asked.

The girls deferred to me.

"I am," I said. I walked across the street and introduced myself (not using my real name, of course). "I haven't seen her in a real long time, and I just thought I'd stop by and catch up."

"I'm cat-sitting while she's down in St. Thomas," the man said.

"St. Thomas?" I smiled. "That's great. Well, if you talk to her, please tell her hi. Do you know when she's coming back?"

He gave me a date sometime the following week, and we parted ways.

With the information he'd unwittingly provided, we were able to nail Sandy. Here's how.

The key was getting Sandy's exact return flight information. If we knew what plane she was on, we'd obviously be in position to trail her when she returned to New York. Even better, with that return flight information, we could arrange to sit next to her on the plane.

Each airline maintains its own computerized reservations system, with every passenger's flight information in it. The rule is, reservations clerks are supposed to access that information only for the passenger or their authorized travel representative.

In the real world, it's a different story.

Posing as Tom Gullickson from Main Street Travel, calling to confirm Sandy's reservation and arrange ground transportation for her, the airlines were only too happy to help me.

When you call an airline to confirm a reservation, they ask you for four pieces of information — the passenger's name, date of travel, city of departure, and flight number. I knew Sandy's name, of course — and her date of travel and departing city from her well-intentioned cat-sitter.

It was easy enough for me to pretend I didn't have the flight information right ("the writing here is kind of smudged," "I left the file in the office, and I'm calling from home" — you get the idea). But I also didn't know which airline she was flying.

Which is where the frequent flyer information I got earlier came in handy. It seemed logical to assume that Sandy would take one of those airlines back from St. Thomas.

As Tom Gullickson, I called those airlines and checked every flight they had that day for Sandy. I got it wrong the first few times — at which point I told the clerk helping me "I'd better double-check my information — I'll call back," and hung up. Then I called that airline's centralized reservations number again and started the same process with a different clerk.

Eventually, I got it right.

When Prudential was apprised of our information, they authorized a trip for an associate and me down to St. Thomas so we could catch Sandy's act in person. We checked every sleeping establishment on St. Thomas and approached every white female at every beach and bar. We eventually found our friend on the nearby island of St. John. A few days later, we were sunning ourselves with Sandy on a luxurious yacht, snorkeling, swimming, dancing at the island nightclubs . . . not activities you'd expect a woman with such a severe and incapacitating case of carpal tunnel syndrome to be capable of.

We even had a video camera along, to tape our little vacation frolics.

Needless to say, when we returned to the U.S., Prudential had little trouble convincing her to drop her claim — and repay what she'd already stolen.

⊔ ⊓ ⊐ ⊐ ⊐

Knowledge of your "behavioral fingerprints" — the fact that you're a comic book fan, that you fly certain airlines — is one tool people in my business use to track you down.

Knowledge of your behavior patterns — what time you go to work, where you drop off your dry cleaning, or where you get your coffee — is another.

PATTY'S MISTAKE

An attorney I knew was representing a man in the middle of a nasty divorce case. During the early years of his marriage, the husband had financed his wife's fledgling business efforts. Her business — brokering the sale of large aircraft (Lear Jets, 747s, 727s, etc.) — had later become incredibly profitable. The wife had a lot of money.

My friend and his client couldn't find a trace of it. They decided to have the wife (her name was Patty) followed. This was not a good idea.

Patty was paranoid.

Being in the middle of a divorce only made matters worse.

Patty lived in Manhattan. Every time she came out of her apartment and saw a car parked nearby, she yelled at the driver to stop following her. If someone innocently looked at her as she walked past, she would stop and scowl at them until they were blocks away. Sometimes, she would scream at completely innocent people, "You're wasting your time. I see you. Leave me alone."

The husband and the attorney went through three different private investigative agencies (whose operatives were among the best in the business) without success. Patty spotted every tail immediately. Like I said . . .

Patty was paranoid.

The investigators were able to establish a number of Patty's behavior patterns. When I was assigned to the case, one immediately caught my eye. She left her apartment very early in the morning, every morning, to walk her dog.

She may have been paranoid, but she didn't suspect the dog and his master who came strolling down her block one morning, Fido sniffing everywhere, the man greedily sucking down coffee from his mug. Though I looked like I'd just rolled out of bed (hair mussed, dressed in an old t-shirt, gray sweatpants, black loafers, and no socks), the dog and I had been up since 4:30 A.M. to be ready for Patty's 7 A.M. appearance.

It was time well spent.

The two dogs exchanged a quick sniff, while Patty and I made brief eye contact and gave short friendly nods.

The following day, the two dogs greeted each other a little more enthusiastically.

Patty and I exchanged smiles and a quick "good morning."

I didn't want to rush our relationship. I let Patty take her time getting comfortable with me. A few days later, she initiated our first conversation.

We talked about our dogs.

A day later, we talked about the weather, then current events and eventually our jobs.

Soon we were talking about her company: how certain countries were easier to conduct business in than others. I always took care not to ask specific, intrusive questions but to make shallow statements to which she could respond.

My client and I had our first clue.

We started investigating banks in those countries for accounts in her name. Within a few weeks, we had the information my client wanted.

❏ ❏ ❏ ❏ ❏

Unfortunately for her, Patty wasn't quite paranoid enough. By walking her dog the same route at the same time every day, she allowed me to become part of the background. A fellow dog-walker, a friendly face — no threat to her at all, simply part of her daily routine.

If she'd varied that routine — occasionally taking a different route with her dog or going out at a different time — she would never have gotten comfortable enough with me to let down her guard.

Once, it became necessary to follow a man who was extremely "hot." A target or suspect is "hot" if he knows he is being monitored. This guy would walk in front of his home each morning with a mug of coffee. He would look up and down the street eyeing every parked car. Over time, he had been very successful exposing those following him.

After he returned to the house, his car would soon emerge from the garage and crawl down the street. A different route each morning. This guy knew how to "cleanse" himself. He would drive in circles, make numerous U-turns, all the while watching and making a mental note of every moving object. The zigzagging paranoia would continue for about a two-mile radius from his home.

Then the strangest thing happened. His cleansing activity itself developed a very unique pattern. He became blind to everything going on around him after he was satisfied that he was clean. He felt safe, secure, and alone at a certain distance from his home. After a couple of miles, this overly cautious, paranoid guy abandoned the most basic measures of security. Once, the driver in the lead car waved wildly at our target just to confirm the startling change of awareness.

We let him have his fun. We eventually got him by using a nine-vehicle team positioned along the major travel routes five miles from his home. We waited for him to come to us.

Be aware. At *all* times.

There are some behaviors we can't change, of course. Some are unvarying by definition: the need to eat, sleep, go to the in-laws for the holidays, etc. Others are basic human needs — the desire for love, sex, power, friendship, and so on.

Those basic instincts are sometimes the easiest of all for investigators to capitalize on. . . .

LUCKY'S BIG BREAK

How would you like having a camera shoved in your face 24 hours a day, 7 days a week, 365 days a year? No matter where you go, whom you're with, or what kind of mood you're in?

Robert De Niro is one of those people who has to deal with the paparazzi everywhere he goes. Newspapers, magazines, and television shows know whatever he does is news, and they're willing to pay top dollar for glimpses into his personal life.

One night at a restaurant in New York, De Niro was being pestered by a particularly obnoxious photographer by the name of 'Lucky' Legiere. Lucky would just not stop interrupting what the actor had intended to be a quiet evening out with friends.

Words were exchanged. Tempers flared.

De Niro allegedly hauled off and slugged the guy.

The actor was arrested. The papers had a field day.

At which point I came into the case, as an unofficial advisor.

"Let's see what Lucky really wants," I suggested.

Surprise — what the photographer wanted was money. Lucky thought he should profit from his experience, according to his Los Angeles-based lawyer.

"We'd like a quarter-million dollars," the man said.

Eventually, Lucky and his lawyer were talked down.

"A hundred thousand dollars — cash — and Lucky doesn't testify against De Niro," the lawyer said. I could hear the drool making its way down his lip.

I could also hear the cell door slamming shut.

Because in their rush to get their hands on De Niro's hundred g's, Lucky and his lawyer had forgotten something very important: It's illegal to accept money to change your testimony in a criminal case.

Greed will do that to you.

It's one of those basic instincts — those basic human needs that you can count on everyone sharing. An instinct that a good investigator — or a con artist — will always try to take advantage of.

In this case, I didn't even have to be that good.

To make matters worse, Lucky's lawyer suggested that the money be picked up by his father who lived in New Jersey. Late that same evening I decided to check this lawyer's father out. I was horrified to discover that he was a retired judge, soon to be innocently sucked into this horrible mess.

To keep that from happening, we scrambled frantically to get the attorney on the next flight to New York — the red-eye from L.A., "Come on, we have to keep this real quiet. The fewer people who know the better. You understand." He grabbed a friend and headed for LAX.

We brought in the Manhattan District Attorney's office, which arranged a limo wired for sound. Lucky's lawyer was met at the airport: The driver then proceeded to pick up Lucky and the hundred g's (which were in, of all things, a plastic Duane Reade shopping bag), and drive to the D.A.'s office downtown.

Lucky and his lawyer opened the limo door expecting to be greeted by officials who would whisk them to the prosecutor's office so they could "change" their criminal complaint against De Niro. Instead, they were met by detectives, who promptly hauled them off to be booked.

I was there, too — with a 35mm camera of my own to capture Lucky's big moment on film. To give him a taste of his own medicine, as it were.

The *New York Post* ran the picture I had taken of Lucky and his lawyer the very next day.

❑   ❑   ❑   ❑   ❑

What do your habits say about you?

And how loudly do they say it?

All the things we've talked about in this chapter — your likes and dislikes, your individual patterns of behavior, and the general behaviors you engage in as a member of the human race — are potential chinks in your protective armor. You might not care if the whole world knows you collect comic books. You might not want them to know you have seventy thousand dollars' worth in your basement.

The only way you'll be able to intelligently evaluate what habits put you at risk is by becoming aware of them. So sit down at your kitchen table, put on the overhead light, and imagine the following scenario.

PLAY DETECTIVE

One cop shuts the door.

The other sits down across the table from you.

"Your fingerprints are on the letter opener," he says.

"Of course they're on the letter opener," you tell him. "It's my letter opener. Somebody took it from my desk."

"You and the deceased didn't get along. You fought all the time."

"All right, we hated each other — that's no secret." The cop regards you impassively. "That doesn't mean I killed him."

A hand comes down your shoulder. You look up at the smiling face of the second cop.

"Hey — maybe you had a good reason. Maybe it was self-defense," the other cop says. You can smell the garlic on his breath. There's a fresh stain — tomato sauce — on his shirt. No secret what kind of food this guy had for dinner.

"Hey, I got to tell you it doesn't look good for you," the first cop says. "Help us out here — tell us what really happened."

"Yeah, help us out," the second cop chimes in. "Jeez, the paperwork we got to fill out if we have to charge you . . ."

"Charge me?" you say. "You mean, as in arrest?" You shake your head. That's the last thing you want. The embarrassment. The shame. The publicity . . . your life will be ruined.

"This is crazy," you tell the first cop, rising up out of your chair. "I wasn't there!"

The cop looks up now. "Really?" he says. "So where were you?"

"Yeah." The second cop puts a yellow legal pad and a pen in front of you. "Give us an alibi."

"An alibi?" you repeat.

"Your whereabouts," the second cop says, leaning over you. "Write 'em down."

The first cop gets up. "Make it a complete record — from the second you woke up till your head hit the pillow. Your whole day. Better yet, do it for every day this past week." He flashes a quick smile. "We'll be back in five."

He and his partner leave the room.

Well?

Write it down.

Start with your Monday morning — *got up at 7, went jogging until 7:30, out of the house at 8:15, drove regular route to work, arrived work at 8:55, lunch at 12* — and go on from there. Do the same for Tuesday, Wednesday, etc. — use a new piece of paper for each day.

Now play detective.

Compare the lists you've written. See any patterns? Or rather . . .

How many patterns do you see? How easy are those patterns for others to spot? Do any of those routines leave you — or your family, your house — vulnerable?

Try this exercise with your spouse, friend, significant other, too. Have them detail your daily routine, and you detail theirs. And if you really want to have fun, casually ask your kids their perception of your daily routine. It will be entertaining and enlightening.

PROTECT YOURSELF

1. Make a list of your behavioral fingerprints. What activities do you need or like to do? What objects do you need or enjoy? Observe how your need or desire reveals information about you. Are you on the mailing list of a newspaper, magazine, or club? Do people refer to you as "the guy with the Dodgers baseball hat" or "the woman with the Armani bag?" Does this "behavioral fingerprint" advertise a potential vulnerability that can be exploited, perhaps by an opening line, an icebreaker? "I love your bag; where'd you get it?" or "Great game last night; did you see that shot in the bottom of the eighth?" Don't become overly paranoid. Just be aware. Only then will you be in control.

2. Exchange and compare behavioral fingerprint lists with a friend. What habits, activities, or desires are the same today as they were five or ten years ago? Can you smell each other coming by a trademark perfume or cologne? Referring to your friend, complete the following sentences: He/She is the one who always wears the _____. You can probably find him/her at _____. Oh, he/she loves _____! Scary, isn't it?

3. Study your daily schedule. Examine it for points of weakness. Do your activities fall into specific, predictable time slots each day? Could you be vulnerable during these times? Is your schedule or to-do list easily reviewed by others or strangers? Can I just look around and determine specifics about

you if I'm a visitor to your office (from the top of your desk) or a repairman walking through your kitchen (countertops, calendars, or refrigerator)? Be wary of new people and circumstances trying to ease into your comfort zone either at work or at home (remember Patty and the dogs). Ask detailed questions about these new people or situations. Don't assume, "Oh, he must be a new employee/neighbor."

4. Vary your routine. Even a slight change to your schedule will keep your predictable actions out of the "like clockwork" category. Go to a different coffee shop. Do your chores on Friday morning instead of Saturday morning. If you feel uneasy or have a particular concern about what happens after you leave your home in the morning, for example, leave and then return unexpectedly a short time later. Leave your house a half-hour before your normal departure time. Review your older relatives' and children's routines, too. Protect them; help them to become more aware. Of course, you don't necessarily have to be concerned that you're the target of an investigation, but you are always at risk for that random circumstance when you become a victim.

5. Make a list of your weaknesses that could be exploited. Does a simple reference to clubs, religions, interests, hobbies cause you to lower your guard? Do the same kind of list for members of your family. Stay alert when someone presses those hot buttons. Do you lower your guard when you're tired or stressed out? In the morning before that second cup of coffee? Can I get your new home address or work telephone number by calling your elderly grandmother and saying I went to school with you? Know which scenarios lower the guard of those who know the most about you — relatives, friends, coworkers. Be sure to tell these people not to give out information, just to be on the safe side. Let everyone know that it's okay to say "Oh, Ed will give you all the information. I'll have him call you as soon as possible." Which basic instincts make you

most vulnerable? The desire for love, sex, power, friendship, money, food, etc.?

6. **Watch out for verbal crowbars.** Con artists often use an innocent opening line to get you to reveal something you shouldn't. Always be prepared for the "turning" question — the one that reveals the real motive. Be ready to shut the conversation down. Does a casual "Nice car!" lead to revealing how many children you have?

7. **Protect your name and address.** Every time you give a company your name and address, find out what they do with them. Insist that all newspapers, magazines, music clubs, etc., get written permission from you before they add your name to a mailing list that is shared with or sold to any other entity. Write on your renewal notices that you won't renew until the company reveals to you what happens to your subscriber data and agrees to get your permission first! The next time one of those little subscriber postcards falls out of a magazine you're reading, write in big letters: "WHERE IS MAILING LIST DISCLOSURE NOTICE?" Then drop the postage-paid postcard in the mail. They'll get the hint.

8. **Watch information about your travel plans.** Demand that your travel arrangements only be discussed with those who possess a confirmation number or special code, such as a PIN. Insist that reservation agents document all inquiries by date and time. If you have a particular concern, call and test them by trying to get information. When you first make your reservations, ask that all subsequent communication only be in writing to a specified address.

9. **Just be aware: Your behavioral fingerprints are everywhere.** Plain fingerprints usually show up only where you've been, but your behavioral fingerprints are constantly spreading at lightning speed. Our goal is not to encourage

paranoia, but to guard against the sinister acts to which we all are vulnerable.

2

YOUR TRASH

THE DAY IT RAINED GARBAGE

I was on my second cup of coffee when I heard it.

A loud, dull thump — the sound a sack of wet cement might make on hitting the ground after a four-story fall.

Since I was sitting on the ground floor of a five-story building at the time, I decided to investigate.

I stepped to the levoured blinds, pulled them aside, and stared out the window at East Sixty-fourth Street.

In case you're not familiar with Manhattan's neighborhoods, this part of the Upper East Side is very upper-crust. The titans of New York society — the Vanderbilts, the Astors, the Whitneys — built their mansions here, virtually all of which are now museums or diplomatic residences/embassies. A block away is the heart of the Madison Avenue shopping district, featuring some of the most exclusive and expensive stores in the world. Bloomingdale's, the quintessential Manhattan store, is just a few short blocks away.

As I gazed out the window at 5 A.M., the last thing I expected to see was the big black plastic bag that flew past me and landed with a resounding smack on the sidewalk. Two other, similar bags were lying there already. I could conclude only one thing.

Here, on the swanky Upper East Side of Manhattan, it was raining garbage.

I set down my coffee on the countertop that had been doubling as my bed for the past month and picked up my car keys.

I was very interested in that garbage.

Let me back up a second. I was sleeping on that countertop because I (and a round-the-clock security force I'd hired) had been assigned by First Fidelity Bank of Philadelphia to protect their investment. Said investment being the townhouse itself — a five-story residence that had stained-glass windows, parquet floors, vaulted ceilings, Jacuzzis, fireplaces, a forty-thousand-dollar alarm system, an atrium, and a private elevator.

This townhouse had previously been home to a crooked financier named Roberto Polo — whose 1988 arrest made the front page of the *New York Times*. Now it was being occupied by two gentlemen of similarly dubious character — Charles Benson Lewis and Nelson Monteleone.

Charles and Nelson had already completely trashed another, somewhat less expensive Philadelphia townhouse the bank owned. In the middle of foreclosure proceedings on that building, they'd threatened to disconnect water pipes, remove lighting fixtures, and deface the property in a thousand other ways. Before they were finally dragged out by the Philadelphia sheriff, they managed to follow through on those threats, causing several hundred thousand dollars' worth of damage.

At which point the bank discovered, to its horror, that Nelson and Charles, under a corporate name, had a mortgage on yet another property: the Sixty-fourth Street townhouse. The bank immediately foreclosed but was terrified the two men were going to damage that building as well. And because of New York City housing laws, which at the time gave tenants virtually every benefit of the doubt in any landlord/tenant dispute, it was impossible for the bank to throw them out of the townhouse. The two men actually harbored dreams of "working something out" with the bank, despite owing millions of dollars.

Which is where I came in.

I tried first to contact Nelson and Charles by phone to discuss the matter rationally. They never answered, and never returned the messages I left them. I went to the townhouse to try to talk face-to-face. No one ever came to the door.

A change of tactics seemed in order.

This dispute was taking place in the middle of one of the harshest winters New York City had seen in many years. So I had First Fidelity fax me a letter designating me as the townhouse's superintendent. The letter further authorized me to enter the building to prevent the pipes inside from freezing.

With that letter and the deed to the property, I brought a locksmith to the townhouse and started drilling the locks on the front door.

Turns out someone was home after all.

Charles (Nelson was in New Orleans at the time) called 911. Within minutes, the cops arrived in response to an urgent "robbery in progress" call.

Needless to say, things got a little tense. Especially when Charles produced a lease.

"I'm a tenant," he said, waving a sheaf of papers at the policemen. "I have rights!"

One of the cops looked at the papers. Then he turned to me.

"It's a lease," the cop said. "The guy's got a lease."

"Let me see that," I replied. I studied the papers for a minute. I'd seen more legitimate three-dollar bills.

The lease was between the corporation Charles and Nelson had set up to buy the townhouse and Charles and Nelson as individual tenants. I knew Charles and Nelson were very clever boys. We were ready for anything. I suspected they'd had it dummied up sometime over the previous week.

But the cops weren't concerned about the details. To them, a lease was a lease — if we wanted to prove it was fraudulent, we should do it in court. So, despite the fact that I had the deed and the paperwork from the building's owners, I was in the wrong.

"You gotta go," one of the cops told us.

I glared at Charles.

"I want to talk to your lawyer," I told him.

The presence of the cops encouraged cooperation. He gave me the number. I took out my cell phone and dialed. When the lawyer came on the phone, we had a heart-to-heart talk during which I asked him if this little lease was worth risking his law license over. Because both of us knew the lease Charles had produced was a fraud.

Not surprisingly, we came to a meeting of the minds.

Charles signed the officer's book indicating that he was permitting us to enter and remain inside the property. This made the cop happy.

The bank was happy too, because now they were able to ensure Charles and Nelson's orderly departure from the townhouse.

Which is how nine cops (three separate shifts, three men on at all times) and I came to be residents of the Upper East Side.

It was actually an easy assignment, for a change. Guys were basically getting paid to sleep, sit around and watch TV, or if they were so inclined, view some of the fabulous artwork Nelson and Charles had on display on the upper floors.

What made the job more memorable were features like the basement's S&M dungeon and the master bedroom's mirrored ceilings. Surely, we were fish out of water. Imagine an overweight, unshaven retired cop sleeping in his underwear in a pink canopied bed, and you begin to get the picture.

Once we got the ground rules straight (we were locked in each night, and Charles and Nelson had to be searched each time they left the building to make sure they weren't leaving with any fixtures that weren't theirs), it appeared the funny games would stop. We were wrong.

Back to the trash.

It was clear after one quick glance that the bags were coming from the townhouse — the fourth floor, in fact, where Charles's bedroom was. So once the bags stopped flying, I went out to the street, where my car was parked out front, and loaded the trunk with whatever it was Charles was so concerned about getting rid of.

Later that night, I opened the bags and checked out my haul.

Bingo. Income tax records and evidence of fraud.

When we informed Charles that we'd "rescued" those documents (I still have a hard time believing he thought throwing them out the window made them any safer) and turned them over to the Philadelphia District Attorney who was ultimately responsible for Charles's fraud conviction, he and Nelson were suddenly in a hurry to pack. Notwithstanding a tantrum over a few chandeliers, they left the Sixty-fourth Street townhouse intact.

❏   ❏   ❏   ❏   ❏

I remember Charles's face at the meeting when we told him about those records he thought he'd thrown out. He was surprised, horrified, and finally angry. "But those are mine!" he shouted.

Uh-uh.

In *California v. Greenwood*, the Supreme Court of the United States ruled that once you place your trash out for disposal, you are relinquishing any rights to it — and are actually displaying it for others to peruse. And use. And abuse.

People like me. Your neighborhood bottle and can collector. That nosy reporter. Your cutthroat corporate competitor. Your worst enemy.

The IRS (or didn't you know that trash was the IRS criminal division's most frequently used information-gathering tool?)

You'll never even know your trash has been examined. Smart garbage pickers will notice what type of trash bags you use and put it in a fresh one after they've completed their work. They'll even duplicate the way you tie the bags. If they don't have the right kind of bag handy, they'll just go searching through the neighbors' trash cans until they find a similar type and color bag — there aren't all that many varieties. Then they replace your bag with your neighbor's. It may make the neighbors a little paranoid, but you won't suspect a thing.

TRASH THE EGO

I was once involved in the king of all trash-bag battles. As the hard-working cleaning staff for a suburban New York three-story office building finished putting out the trash one evening, operatives from three different government agencies prepared to pounce on the day's evidence. The routine was well rehearsed as this had been going on for a few weeks. Government vans and various unmarked vehicles quietly revved up as the cleaning couple threw the last remaining bags of office trash in the dumpster just before they went home for the night. You could hear everyone's medical gloves snapping as the vehicles raced to the dumpster. Grown men — all working for the same federal government — literally fighting over bags of garbage.

Do not — ever — underestimate the power of trash! You leave trash behind more frequently than you leave fingerprints. And trash provides much more information. Chances are you'll never really know that your trash has been, as we say in the business, "recovered," because it's an ego thing.

Let me explain.

Investigators, more often than not, refer to their findings as "evidence collected for information purposes." This means that how they got the information will probably never be revealed. For example, let's say you have a hidden lover/bank account/property in a state two thousand miles away from where you live. You've done a pretty good job of covering your tracks, but the slightest bit of information from your trash about the out-of-state "asset" could point to where someone should look for the proverbial needle in the haystack.

I don't know one federal agent who would replace the mystique of James Bond-like sleuthing with the realities of the dirty work. I'm referring, of course, to poking through a week's worth of diapers in a dumpster.

A nameless FBI agent I know shared with me his horror of almost being exposed as a garbage picker. He was alone behind a small business complex late one evening. Although it was a seedy part of town, he stood proudly inside a medium-size trash container, picking and poking — searching for gold. A penlight was clenched between his teeth. He was fully engrossed in the coffee-stained financial papers held between his gloved hands. All of a sudden, some thug appears out of nowhere under a light, coming straight at him. My friend/federal agent/garbage man can't discern what the guy has in his hands but things are not looking too good. He keeps his cool. The next day's head-lines are racing through his head: THUG ATTACKS FBI AGENT IN TRASH BIN. He'll be known around the world as the Dumpster G-man — as in Garbage man. He's convinced his wife will divorce him. Now this guy's smart, good under pressure. He quickly draws his gun and badge. "FBI! Don't move!" he shouts. The thug stops cold in his tracks, but my friend can't take this guy in. The defense attorney will have a field day in court.

"Turn around . . . slowly," he says sternly, "Now go, go away. Get out of here. Just keep walking and don't look back."

The thug is convinced he's going to get shot in the back, "No, no, please." The G-man yells, "Just get out of here! Go!" The thug scampers off. J. Edgar Hoover would've been proud.

A few years ago I was trying to get a friend of mine — Paula — to get a friend of hers — Mabel — to go out with me on a date. Mabel was not interested. Finally, Paula confessed: "There's no way in hell she'll ever go out with you. You pick garbage."

I need to telephone Mabel. I have a friend she might want to meet. He's a doctor. A proctologist. (Mabel is, believe it or not, a book critic for the *New York Times*. God help me!)

Where should you throw out your trash, especially those things that could come back to haunt you later, like detailed income information, bank statements, very personal correspon-dence, the diary where you recorded every unreported penny you made trading baseball cards? Those private, personal documents that just wouldn't look good in the light of day?

Play it safe. Discard sensitive material someplace other than your home. Take it to the dump. Take it to a friend's house (the IRS agent after your financial records will never look in your buddy's garbage). Put it in a small garbage bag and take it on your next road trip. Or throw it out in sections: a third at work, a third on the road, a third at home. Don't leave all the pieces to the puzzle in the same container! All too often, people do the double or triple rip when they discard confidential paperwork. This only highlights the paper that needs to be reassembled for a closer review. I've watched highly successful men and woman crawl across conference tables, eager to help piece together critical parts of an information puzzle.

Or rip the paper into small pieces and flush it down the toilet (if someone recovers your discarded papers from the sewer lines, he deserves to find what he's looking for).

Some of the more concerned (more accurately stated: paranoid) government operatives I know use one of a few chemical compounds that literally disintegrates their important papers without a trace.

You can make your own little home paranoia kit with a small quantity of bleach and a bucket of water. Drop the offending piece of paper in and wait a few minutes. All markings will be erased, and you can pour the inky water down the drain.

Keep in mind it's not just the important papers you throw out that give away information about you. What does that new Gateway computer box sitting at the curb tell the neighborhood — and everyone who happens to be passing through?

BEHOLD THE POWER OF CHEESE

American. Asiago. Brie.

Pizza, lasagna, nachos, burritos, chimichangas, and tacos.

Camembert, cheddar, mozzarella, Muenster, Parmesan,

Roquefort, Stilton, and Swiss.

The Egg McMuffin.

Cheese is big business. According to the National Dairy Council, Americans consume almost six billion pounds of it per year — about two hundred pounds for every man, woman, and child.

A great deal of that business is in the low-fat marketplace. The big companies — and the little ones — are all scrambling around, trying to find that better-tasting, low-calorie product. Pulling out the fat, though, means pulling out the flavor. To add back taste, companies use a fat substitute.

One of the most popular is a chemical compound developed by Monsanto under the name Simplesse®. This natural dairy ingredient is used in low-fat baked goods, creamers, sour cream, etc., to enhance creaminess and mimic the taste of fat.

Monsanto makes this product by the truckload and happily sells it to companies all across the world. They've got a patent on it, of course — one they exert their best efforts to protect.

In 1991, I became part of those best efforts.

Monsanto executives got wind that the San Diego-based Corona cheese company was about to bring a new low-fat cheese product to the marketplace. Monsanto suspected Corona was using Simplesse in their new cheese. I was brought in to obtain samples of the product and evidence of its manufacture.

Which is how I came to be standing in the middle of a multi-acre cheese factory, wearing a three-piece suit and bandying about terms like "fat mimetic," "microparticulated whey concentrate," and "enhanced dairy characteristics."

The business cards in my wallet identified me as Daniel Johnson, sales rep for Dorvalle Import/Export. I was touring Corona's facilities in advance of placing a big order for my company. As a visiting VIP, I was getting the red-carpet treatment from Corona executives, including the company's executive vice-president Diane Ruano — who also happened to be the boss's daughter.

I'd made my deal just big enough that the elder Ruano ("Please! You must call me Francisco!") had already called in to make sure

I was happy and to say how sorry he was that we wouldn't have the chance to meet. He hoped our two companies would establish a "mutually beneficial relationship" over the next few years.

I made all the right noises back at him: how impressive Corona's factory was, how Diane was giving me the red-carpet treatment, and that I hoped we would do a lot of business together, too.

"Everything looks great," I told Diane. "I need to make a few calls," implying I needed to finalize the big order. "Can I use a phone?"

"Sure," she said. She marched me off the plant floor and into her father's office. Walking behind his fine cherry-wood desk, she pulled out his leather chair, smiled up at me, and said, "make yourself at home."

She even shut the door behind her on the way out.

For a minute, I thought I'd died and gone to heaven.

Monsanto had hired me to find out what the Corona cheese company was up to, and now I was sitting at the desk of the company president. His inbox was overflowing with memos, faxes, and important-looking scraps of paper. A neatly arranged stack of phone messages sat next to the phone. On the far wall, Francisco Ruano's portrait hung over a long row of filing cabinets.

It was too good to be true.

I immediately suspected I was being monitored via closed-circuit TV.

I decided not to touch anything. Instead, I called my associates in New York, and after using a prearranged code to sweep the line for bugs, started whispering the contents of everything on the president's desk. Bills of lading, inventory, interoffice memos — anything that I could see, I read into the phone, all the while acting as I thought a salesman should when calling in to the home office. Pacing back and forth, waving my hands about, laughing — you get the idea.

It was during one particularly long round of pacing that I spied the document shredder. It was in the corner of his office.

Not a surprise to see a shredder there — industry analysts

estimate that the market for shredders is growing between 50 and 60 percent a year. They're virtually standard equipment in every corporate office, and you'll find them in more and more small businesses and home offices as well.

You can trace at least part of this growth to the explosion of computer databases. More paperwork is being generated that contains private information. People don't trust that the private information is safe in their regular trash. So, they think —

"Let's get a shredder. That'll keep them from pulling our bank statement out of the garbage."

Well . . .

Funny thing about document shredders, especially the cheaper models, which is what Francisco Ruano had purchased: As you feed the documents you wish to consign to oblivion into the shredder, they emerge as nice little ribbons of paper, which fall in neat rows into the garbage, one on top of the other.

Very easy to reconstruct.

Start by placing several long strips of scotch tape, sticky side up, on a table. Then carefully pick up one layer of the shredded paper from the wastebasket and lay it flat on the table.

Repeat the process until you have the whole document.

The farther down into the garbage you go, the easier this gets to do, because the paper's all been compressed into easily identifiable layers. Sometimes you catch a break, and your target has shredded a variety of paper that day — different stock, colors, patterns — which makes the papers even easier to reconstruct.

A quick look inside Francisco Ruano's garbage revealed several different kinds of paper. I added to the mess by tossing in a wrapper from a Hershey bar I'd gotten in the vending machine on the warehouse floor. Then I finished up my phone call and stepped outside the office.

Diane was waiting for me with a big basket of cheese — a gift sampler of all of Corona's different products.

"You're too kind," I told her.

I took the sampler and promised to phone her with confirmation of our order the next day.

Seven hours later, I was in their dumpster, poking a hand through various garbage bags, looking for a bag of shredded paper with a Hershey bar wrapper in it. It didn't take me too long to find.

I stopped off at a 7-Eleven, bought several rolls of scotch tape, and went to work reconstructing the documents from Ruano's shredder — using the exact method I discussed above.

Sometime just before dawn, I found myself staring at a reconstructed bill of lading for a shipment into Corona's San Diego plant. Ten fifty-five-gallon drums of something labeled only "fat substitute."

Next to that bill of lading was another — ten fifty-five-gallon drums of Simplesse, shipped from Monsanto direct to a warehouse just inside the Mexican border.

Corona was buying Simplesse in Mexico, relabeling it at their Mexican warehouse, and shipping it into the United States for use in testing their low-fat cheese product.

Monsanto filed suit. Corona was forced to purchase Simplesse from Monsanto's U.S. subsidiaries — at a considerably higher cost.

Mr. Ruano, as I mentioned, had a cheap shredder — one that only cuts paper lengthwise. If you buy a shredder, spend the money and get a cross-cut shredder, one that reduces your paper into small bits of confetti.

Consider this, though: The shredded document in the case above turned out to be worth millions of dollars to Monsanto.

Even if it had been chopped into tiny pieces and mixed in with day-old egg salad, it would have been worth my time to put it back together.

If someone is motivated enough, they'll spend the time to reconstruct your shredded trash.

IT'S A GIRL!

Everyone in the crowded elevator smiled.

The little girl I held in my arms was sound asleep, her head on my shoulder. Her peaceful smile had touched everyone.

A pretty woman with long, dark hair, positioned behind a baby stroller, stroked Johanna's hair and smiled up at me as well. My wife, Deb.

Our loving family unit.

The elevator chimed and opened onto the forty-second floor.

"Excuse us," I said, leading the way off the elevator and into an elegantly appointed waiting room belonging to the law firm of Johnson, Jacoby, and Meldridge. It held a long, brown leather couch, two coffee tables piled high with magazines, and several comfortable chairs.

I hung up our coats and positioned a few Winnie the Pooh books beside us.

Johnson, Jacoby, and Meldridge occupied five floors of this forty-five-story building. One floor above us was the law firm's main reception area — with not one, but two receptionists. Here, there was only the desk across from us, with a phone and a phone directory sitting on it — to be used, obviously, to contact the person you were there to see.

Johanna opened her eyes, excited to see Winnie the Pooh. "Can you read to me?" she asked as she nestled her head against my chest.

Deb picked up one of the magazines and sat down in a chair.

While I was reading about Pooh and Piglet and their plan to build poor Eeyore a house of his own, and a particularly bouncy Tigger, I kept one eye focused on the door leading into the law firm's offices.

Just as Eeyore was telling Pooh how he really fell in the water, the door swung open, and two men, very much in a hurry, charged through. One of them barely gave us a second look. The other stopped.

"Can I help you?" he asked.

"That's okay," Deb said. "We're waiting for someone."

"All right," the man said. "Good night."

"Good night," Deb replied.

My attention was focused less on their conversation than on the brief glimpse I got of a long hallway, lined with offices, before the door swung shut again. One of those offices belonged to a man named John Stannis.

Stannis was part of a conglomerate that was buying smaller companies, filtering their profits through corporate shells, and running them into the ground. There was fraud involved to the tune of tens of millions of dollars. But Stannis knew the ins and outs of the legal system. We couldn't prove anything from the legal papers he'd filed.

We needed the papers he wasn't filing.

We needed his trash.

But getting at it without being arrested for trespassing was going to be a problem. The interior hallways near the service elevators were covered by video cameras, as were the loading docks where the garbage trucks came to pick up the trash every night.

We'd had people in and out of Stannis's office over the past week — lost telephone repairmen, restaurant delivery people — all of them studying the law firm's trash-collection procedures. Finally, we'd found a weak spot.

It was just after 5:30. More employees were starting to leave. As one woman laden down with a briefcase and several shopping bags full of file folders started to squeeze through the door, I got up and held it open for her.

"Thank you," she said, and then she glanced at Johanna. "What a cute little girl."

"Thank you," I replied.

As she turned to go, I picked up the doorstopper next to the couch and propped the door open.

The hallway was now visible from where I sat. And about ten minutes later, so was the weak spot we'd discovered in the law firm's trash collection procedures: the cleaning woman.

She walked out of one office, dropped a small black plastic bag on the floor, then walked into the next office. Later, another worker would come by to collect all the bags in the hall.

Johanna had now fallen back asleep. I closed the book and stood. I gently placed Johanna in Deb's arms and reached for the stroller. "Daddy's got trash to pick," I'm thinking to myself.

The cleaning woman walked into Stannis's office.

I took our coats and proceeded to push the stroller down the hallway.

The cleaning woman reappeared, dropped Stannis's trash on the floor, and went on to the next office to clean.

When I passed Stannis's office, I reached down with one hand, placed his trash in the stroller, and dropped our coats on top of it.

At the end of the hallway, I turned around.

On our way out, we said goodnight to the cleaning woman. Then we walked to the elevator and left the building without incident. The security guards, careful not to awaken Johanna, waved and whispered, "Good night."

After treating my family to dinner at a nice Italian restaurant on Lexington Avenue — and thanking them for their help — I returned to my office, a bachelor again.

I spread Stannis's trash out on my desk.

It didn't take long to find what I was looking for. Faxes, memos, and bank transfers: a paper trail that led us — and the authorities — to the millions of dollars in illegitimate profits Stannis and his associates had accumulated.

❑ ❑ ❑ ❑ ❑

What you throw away at work may reveal as much — if not more — about you than what you throw away at home. Getting that business trash presents some special problems, though, because of the way it's collected. Even if the law says I have a right to look at it once you throw it out, you're hardly going to invite me into the building to do so.

Sometimes — as in the case above — you have to get a little creative.

Sometimes, you just have to dive right in that dumpster.

Those dives, though they often have an aromatic downside, can be entertaining.

Like the time I discovered a cop and an FBI agent, hip-deep in trash, holding guns on each other. Or the raccoon I surprised, hard at work on trash he considered vitally important. I don't know who was more scared, but I do know that I now make sure no animals are around *before* I hop in a container.

If you run a business, consider what's going out with your trash.

A gentleman named Bruce James, late of Philadelphia, currently residing in a federal penitentiary, used the information he and four cohorts found in dumpsters outside of banks to order new checks for seventy-five different banking accounts. They turned those checks into close to a quarter-million dollars' worth of cash.

Be careful with your ATM slips, which sometimes have your account number printed on them, and, if not, always provide leads to it.

Be careful with everything you throw out in public, even the notes you scrawl to yourself while waiting in line at the movies or standing at a public phone. Change them before you throw them away — provide a little misinformation. Use shorthand or a code that only you understand.

You never know where that paper will end up.

WHAT COULD BE DONE

There are a great many people uncomfortable with the law regarding trash right now — including members of the Supreme Court that helped establish it. Why? In his dissenting opinion, the late Justice William J. Brennan put the matter rather succinctly:

"Scrutiny of another's trash is contrary to commonly accepted notions of civilized behavior. I suspect, therefore, that members of our society will be shocked to learn that the Court, the ultimate guarantor of liberty, deems unreasonable our expectation that the aspects of our private lives that are concealed safely in a trash bag will not become public."

It may seem somewhat hypocritical for me to be saying this (after all, I've gotten paid good money over the years to paw through trash), but I happen to agree with Justice Brennan. You should be able to throw something out without having to worry whether people will be pawing through it the second you set it down on the curb.

Here's how it could be done: You hire the handler of your trash (your local government or a private hauler) to act as your agent in protecting your private material. Just like engaging the services of a delivery company. They'd agree not to review, distribute, or otherwise make it available to anyone else. They could possibly set up "print bleaching" containers for private papers to be cleansed and prepared for recycling.

If the police caught someone out on the curb going through your garbage, the local D.A. would have a case he could really sink his teeth into. Your contract with your trash hauler would address the issue that you've "abandoned" your trash. You would be simply placing your items for pick-up by your authorized agent — and protector or guardian of your personal information.

A FINAL WORD

So your trash made it safely to the landfill. It's gone now, buried forever beneath a mountain of other garbage. That incriminating diary/letter/income tax information will never see the light of day.

Not so fast, Charlie.

Most landfills are more organized than your desktop. That featureless mountain of trash is actually a meticulously arranged grid, mapped out in vertical and horizontal sectors. Every sector is dated as it fills, and the source of the trash contained therein is recorded.

If I know you threw away something the week of January 15, I know where in the landfill to look for it.

It'll be tough, sure — kind of like looking for a needle in a haystack. But again, if my motivation is strong enough, I'll spend the time searching for it.

It's my firm suspicion that the evidence that could have convicted O.J. Simpson of murdering his ex-wife and Ron Goldman is sitting somewhere in the Los Angeles city dump. I'm talking, of course, about the missing bag — the one that O.J. had, and then didn't have, at the airport. The one with the knife and the bloody clothes.

The Los Angeles Police Department could have saved a hell of a lot of time and money if they'd just recovered that bag. Might have taken them a few weeks with the proper manpower and planning. In fact, I'll bet it could still be found: probably in pretty good shape, since it's no doubt in a plastic (never-decaying) trash bag. If they want volunteers, I'd be right in line — after the Goldmans and the Browns.

Remember the excitement when they cracked open Al Capone's vaults a few years back? Live television special, hosted by Geraldo Rivera? Surely the same kind of energy could be generated for new evidence in the Trial of the Century. They could try O.J. again, technically not for murder — that would be double jeopardy, but they could charge him on federal charges for violating Nicole Brown's and Ron Goldman's civil rights. This could be done in either California or Illinois — where he fled after the murder. Big ratings.

Fox Television, are you listening?

PLAY DETECTIVE

First of all, thank me for not asking you to wade through the dumpster outside your local twenty-four-hour convenience store to complete this particular exercise.

You're welcome.

Now, pick one of the following:

- Kinko's.
- Staples.
- The post office.

Let's say you chose Kinko's — that document management store that has grown from a single Isla Vista, California, store-front in 1970 to a chain with close to one thousand locations nationwide. A lot of smaller businesses/independent business people now use their local Kinko's as an extension of their physical office space. They send/receive faxes there, mail FedEx packages, design advertising/promotional pieces, make copies, and utilize their waste-disposal services.

That is, their trash cans.

Your assignment is to walk into your local Kinko's, walk over to one of those trash cans (keeping your head up), and without batting an eye, reach in and pull out a stack of paper.

I guarantee you'll find information in there someone wanted kept confidential.

A resume, certainly. A business plan, perhaps. A juicy proposal.

You can take the assignment a step further, if you'd like. Do some comparison shopping; try this out at Kinko's, Staples, *and* your local post office.

Kinko's may have more resumes in its garbage than Staples.

The post office will no doubt have more personal and business correspondence than either. Just think of the mail some people throw out without even opening the envelope!

Now turn the exercise around: What have you thrown away at Kinko's, assuming it was safely discarded?

PROTECT YOURSELF

1. **Become trash-conscious.** Be aware of what you're throwing out at the bank, at the post office, on an airplane, at

the gas station, at home, at work. Develop procedures to securely dispose of important papers. Business owners and managers should also conduct a trash review of every department and worker on a regular basis. Take a moment and think about what you discard at your curb. What do these items reveal about you and your family? Imagine that you threw out a winning lottery ticket. Do you think you'd find it? Do you think you'd piece it together even if it went through a shredder? Do you think you'd find a way to extract that ticket even if it had been eaten by a neighborhood dog?

2. Get a crosscut (confetti-type) shredder. Throw out all other shredders. Examine your paper rip profile. Do you rip important papers two or three times thinking you've provided some degree of confidentiality? Or, are you the type that rips documents into smaller pieces? Remember, ripped pieces reveal a conscious or unconscious desire to hide something. Consider shredding *all* documents. Otherwise shredding simply points to the important papers. Some people may want to use the bleach method for very private printed matter. Place your important papers in a bucket of water containing a half-cup of bleach.

3. Compile a trash profile on a family member or coworker using their trash. Show them what their trash reveals about them — personal information, buying habits, vacation plans, financial records, etc.

4. Without touching any trash, walk around your office and your home and just look (no touching) into any trash bin. What can you see? A bank statement? Addresses, personal information, phone numbers, to-do lists, doodlings, reminders, etc.?

5. Practice the art of misinformation. Hand-written notes to yourself can contain valuable information for someone monitoring the trash can next to a pay phone. Change some of

the facts on very private notes. If you have a phone number written down, change it before you throw it out. Turn 3s into 8s, 1s into 4s: be aware of what you're advertising in the trash.

3

YOUR PUBLIC PROFILE

THE LEAKY CASKET CAPER

Chances are, if someone you know died recently, he or she was buried in a Batesville casket. The Indiana-based company (www.batesville.com) is the country's leading coffin manufacturer, making over five hundred different kinds of caskets that range in cost from $600 to $29,000 and in style from a simple pine box to a virtually indestructible bronze casket.

Without going into all the gory details, as the body in a coffin decomposes, fluids pool at the base and eventually evaporate. Every coffin — no matter what the cost — has a pan at the base to help collect these fluids and prevent them from leaking out.

Sometimes fluids will seep through the casket. Usually it's not a problem, because the majority of the time, the casket is underground. But if the burial is above ground, in a mausoleum, any sort of leak can get a little messy. In 1963, Batesville began offering an insured warranty on all their caskets, providing additional peace of mind and protection for those families choosing hardwood caskets and mausoleum interment.

In 1983, a man named Tomas Skorzy alleged that the Batesville casket he'd purchased for a recently deceased family member had failed. Fluids had leaked all over the family mausoleum. Stone and marble needed to be replaced. Emotional distress had been inflicted. Skorzy wailed and threatened to go the media.

He asked for a million dollars.

Batesville settled the claim quickly — without going to court, without examining the physical evidence in detail — for a six-figure sum.

Almost ten years later, a woman named Ilena Vargas made a very similar claim. She, however, wanted ten million dollars. Again, there was intense pressure to settle quickly. Vargas threatened to go to the local and national media with her story.

This is where I came in.

Batesville executives wanted to find out if the similarities to the previous claim were accidental, and if there was any merit to her case.

Initially, all we had to go on were Vargas's name and telephone number. Through phone company records, we got her address — a building on Manhattan's Upper East Side, with several particularly attentive doormen.

We tried a number of different ruses to get past them ("Pizza delivery," "I'm here to see my friend," "I'm collecting for the ASPCA") — all without success. What finally worked was my stumbling into the building late one Saturday night, posing as a resident, pretending to be more than a little drunk. A mumbled hello as I walked past the night doorman, my keys out and jingling in my hand, and I was on the elevator.

Once on her floor, I headed not towards Vargas's apartment, but straight for the end of the hall. My destination: the trash room, where that floor's residents discarded their garbage. For pick-up by the building's maintenance staff, they assumed.

But also, as per the U.S. Supreme Court, for perusal by any and all interested parties. Such as myself.

Her discarded utility bill quickly identified Ilena's trash — a small white plastic bag, which I brought back to my office to examine more closely.

Besides that bill, her trash contained a half-eaten salami sandwich, an empty aspirin bottle, and a small brown paper bag. In the bag was a stack of receipts for various postal money orders — about forty in all.

I spread the receipts out on my kitchen table.

Each receipt listed the name of the payor (the person who bought the money order), the payee (the person who was receiving it), and the amount of the money order. The amounts ranged from twenty-five to five hundred dollars. The payees were all different too, with addresses ranging up the eastern seaboard, from Florida to Maryland.

There were a number of different payors as well — Vargas was one. Her name, in fact, was repeated on half a dozen slips.

Curious. Why would Vargas have all these receipts for money orders different people bought? Was she someone's bookkeeper?

I looked a little closer.

And saw that the handwriting on all of them was the same. Every one of those money orders had been bought by Ilena Vargas . . .

If that was even her real name.

Time to find out a little more about Ms. Ilena Vargas.

Time to start checking public records.

The term is self-explanatory — a public record is a document available for the general public to review. The government — local, county, state, and federal — begins assembling a file of those documents containing information on you the moment you're born.

Government archives are the major source of public record documents.

What's in those archives? Your mortgage. Your property tax bill. Your birth certificate. Any kind of permits, agreements, passports, licensing applications, and motor vehicle records (a special case, which we'll cover in the next chapter). Your marriage certificate, your voter registration card (which for the benefit of all the would-be forgers out there, has your signature on it), as well as copies of virtually every kind of lawsuit you've ever been involved in — divorces, criminal cases, court actions, judgments, liens, etc. All available to the general public to look over, either for free or for a nominal fee.

Publicly available government records like these are the first weapon in every investigator's arsenal. And a special treat for con men.

On the leaky casket caper, we had local law enforcement run the payee names and addresses — as well as Vargas and the other payors — through every public record available to them.

We struck gold.

The names on Vargas's money orders were connected to each other in a trail of paperwork a mile long — a web of property records, shell corporations, and false identities. When we sat down and sorted it all out, we found an extended family of criminals (gypsies, actually), engaged in a pattern of fraudulent activities up and down the East Coast.

Among the scams they'd run was Skorzy's fraudulent claim against Batesville.

Among the mistakes they'd made was having Vargas's elder brother pay the property taxes on Skorzy's elegant new home, which he'd apparently purchased with the 1983 settlement money from Batesville.

A connection between the two lawsuits firmly established, Batesville was able to deny Vargas's claim unequivocally. We then happily assisted local enforcement agencies in rounding up the people involved in the other fraudulent activities.

PRIVATE AFFAIRS

Sure, they're not "official" public records . . .

But there are numerous circumstances under which even your most personal, private papers can become subject to public scrutiny.

On a recent trip through Vermont, I stopped at an antiques store just outside of Montpelier. In a barn full of old furniture and vintage clothes, I found a shoebox filled with letters dated from 1934.

They were all from a soldier, desperately trying to convince a young lady to marry him. "This is living history," I marveled to myself as I read. "Look at how these people talked back then, the way they wrote. What beautiful handwriting he had." It was fascinating — for me.

But what about that soldier?

I bet lover boy would be spinning in his grave to learn these very private letters from him to his girlfriend were sitting in a shoebox next to some old dishes and rusting utensils, available for public inspection.

So what's in that shoebox buried in the back of your closet?

Make believe you're going to be departing this world one week from now. Is there something around on your hard drive or in the back of a desk drawer that you wouldn't want that special person in your life to see? Get rid of it.

Are there things in your office at work that, if discovered, would lead to similarly embarrassing situations? Get rid of them, too.

Imagine that the *National Enquirer* was given full lawful access to everything of yours at your death. In fact, its reporters are walking into your home as the cops are wheeling your corpse out the door. What would you prefer they not feature on the cover of their next issue? You just might hope that there isn't life after death to avoid the potential embarrassment.

Embarrassment not just for you, but for your family, your business, for everyone connected with you who will survive after you're gone.

Keep your private affairs private by not leaving a record of
them for others to find.

BIG BROTHER

Your public record begins with a birth certificate and ends with
your last will and testament — available for review (in most
locales) at the surrogate court clerk's office. The government is
filling in the space between those bookends with an ever-
increasing amount of documentation on you.

To coin a phrase . . .

Big Brother is not only watching, he's taking notes.

Make sure he's not writing down the wrong information.

Pick up the phone book, find the phone numbers for your
local government offices — the municipal clerk, the county clerk,
the surrogate clerk — and start calling them. Find out which
records their specific offices maintain. Then go down to those
offices in person and see what the records have to say about you
and your family. Make sure the information is correct — errors
can spread quickly from one public database to another and take
a tremendous amount of effort to fix.

(If you've got Internet access, you can do some of your home-
work on-line. Check our resources list for more details.)

Once you've dealt with your local bureaucracy, take a day or
two off. Treat yourself to a night on the town.

Then make another round of calls to the state, and federal,
government offices.

Of course, the government — in particular, the federal government — maintains whole buildings of records on you that are
not open to the public for review. The Freedom of Information
Act entitles you to look at many of them upon request. It's worth
taking the time to do so. In particular, make sure to get a copy
of your Social Security Earnings Statement. Call 800-772-1213 to
have one sent to you.

If the information in that isn't right, turn immediately to the section on identity theft on page 203.

Otherwise, keep reading.

CONSPIRACY THEORY

The gentleman sitting across the conference room table from me was named Andrew Topping. In his three-piece suit, red bow tie, and starched white shirt, he looked every inch the Harvard professor he was — chairman of the Sanskrit department, in fact.

Yet Topping was having trouble answering a simple question. So I repeated it.

"Have you ever been arrested?" I asked.

Topping — a man who resembled, more than anything else, a miniature version of Groucho Marx — fidgeted in his chair and glanced around the table nervously.

Topping, on the recommendation of one of his colleagues who had connections to the CIA, had come to consult us (me and two associates I was working with at the time) on a matter "of utmost urgency." He was apparently in business with someone whom he distrusted and wanted that person monitored. We'd recommended meeting in person to discuss the situation.

The tone of our conversation was no doubt somewhat different than he'd expected.

We started the meeting off by saying that when we took on a case, we wanted to know everything about it that could be relevant, which included background information on our potential client(s).

"Just so there aren't any surprises if things get nasty — is there anything in your past you need to share with us?" I asked.

Topping, who was happily munching on one of the doughnuts I'd set out in the middle of the table, quickly shook his head and took a sip of coffee.

"Any altercations with anyone, any big lawsuits in the past or currently pending?" I continued.

Topping shook his head again.

"Okay," I said. Then I leaned forward and simultaneously lowered my voice.

"Professor Topping — have you ever been arrested?"

As I said above, I had to repeat the question before Topping finally answered.

"Well . . . ," he said, his face coloring slightly. "It was all poppycock. Absolute poppycock."

"Why don't you tell us about it?" I prompted, exchanging knowing glances with my associates.

Not that he really needed to. I just wanted the professor to get used to telling us the whole truth if we were going to go to work for him. His criminal record we knew about already.

"I was arrested for conspiracy," Topping said.

"To do what?" I asked.

"Just conspiracy," he said, folding his arms against his chest.

"Professor," I said, "we need to have all the necessary background information first — you can understand that, surely? So, you were arrested for conspiracy. Conspiracy to do what? And with whom?"

I didn't blame him for being reluctant to reveal the details, but as I said above, I wanted him to trust us.

Topping cleared his throat.

"Well," he said, "what they charged me with was conspiracy to assassinate the president — Nixon, at the time. But as I said, it was all poppycock. . . ."

And he went off again, talking about how the charges had been blown out of proportion and how innocent he was.

Topping was a bit of a character. I'd guessed as much the night he first called us (he sounded more than a little paranoid over the phone), but because of his connections, we were reluctant to believe anything bad about him.

Still, I had thought it worthwhile taking a little time to check him out before we met. But when I finally cleared enough off my desk to spend a moment on Topping, it was already close to midnight. Our meeting was the next morning at 9 A.M. How could I run that detailed background check I needed on Topping in time?

By turning on my computer and logging onto the Internet.

I got background information on Topping — as well as the lowdown on his arrest — from a public record database: a searchable site of newspaper articles. One of the biggest of these is Lexis-Nexis (**www.lexis-nexis.com**). It maintains close to nine thousand separate databases of information, from newspapers, magazines, court decisions, and government archives. It's a by-subscription service — but many public libraries have purchased access to it. So has virtually every law firm.

Companies such as Merlin Information Systems are another source of information for investigators (**www.merlindata.com**).

Merlin has purchased many of the public records mentioned above from the government and entered them into proprietary database form — available for access via the Internet. You can search databases like California property records, for example, and find out who owns that house next to your uncle's in Encino by simply entering the address.

Merlin also offers a number of public record CD-ROMs for sale, like the *TriStatePeople Finder*. This will let you search through a complete list of Connecticut, New Jersey, and New York State residents by last name — and give you their last three known addresses.

Neither Merlin nor Lexis-Nexis has the field to itself, of course. See our resources list at the back of the book for places to find more companies mining the same area.

Since these new firms sprang into existence, I don't have to drive down to the county courthouse as often or spend as much time at the library as I used to, going through microfilms of old newspapers. My life is easier. Yours, on the other hand . . .

An old boyfriend can track down where you live.

A stranger can see what property you own.

A potential employer can check out your criminal record.

Think about how much information is out there in those databases, available to anyone with a few clicks of the mouse.

Think about what happens when that information is wrong.

Bronti Kelly was an experienced retail salesman who suddenly had difficulty finding a job. This difficulty lasted four years.

Kelly finally discovered that the Stores Protective Association — a nonprofit group that provides background information to retail chains — had been circulating an erroneous shoplifting report about him. He had to change his name and social security number and start his life all over again.

❏ ❏ ❏ ❏ ❏

What finally happened with Topping?

After we finished the job he hired us for, I referred him to a lawyer I knew for another problem he had. She helped him out, and he promptly disappeared. Without paying her.

So if you know where Professor Andrew Topping, late of Harvard University, is, please do contact me. I'd like to get my friend her money. And Professor, if you're out there and having an attack of conscience, feel free to send a check for the amount you still owe your lawyer to me, c/o Longstreet Press.

THE LEAKY BASEMENT CAPER

If you find yourself cruising down Interstate 95 through the southwestern part of Connecticut, take a moment from your drive and pull off Exit 33. You'll be right on a town line. On one side of that boundary is Bridgeport, the classic blue-collar town, fallen (frankly) on hard times. On the other side is Fairfield — home to some of the finest houses in the region.

Now the line between the two towns has gotten a little bit fuzzy. In fact, the single largest piece of private property in Bridgeport is right on that town line. On that property is a mansion literally the size of a school. God only knows how many bedrooms and bathrooms are in it.

If you stand at the gates guarding the mansion from the main road and look down the long driveway, the odds are pretty good you'll see at least part of the owner's extensive car collection. Perhaps his antique Mercedes, or his Rolls Royce — he's got hundreds.

The owner is a man named Peter Hartman, one of the richest men I've ever come across in my life. And one cheap bastard.

How do I know this? Because of the eight long years of my life it took to track him down and satisfy a legal judgment for a client.

My client was a man named Paul Goodyear — an upstanding citizen, pillar of his local business and financial community, and the founder and president of the New Rochelle Academy, a very prominent private school in New Rochelle, New York. In the late 1980s, Dr. Goodyear sold one of the school's buildings — its former commissary — to Peter Hartman. Hartman planned to convert the single-story, concrete block structure into a storage facility for a portion of his antique car collection.

Hartman, however, didn't want to give Goodyear the money he owed him. And despite repeated attempts to resolve the dispute without going to court, Goodyear was eventually forced to foreclose and get back the deed to the property . . .

Which was when his problems really began.

Hartman had never bothered to pay taxes on the property when he owned it. As the deed-holder, Goodyear now found himself in the hole for tens of thousands of dollars to the state and local taxmen. Worse, because Hartman never bothered to perform even the most basic maintenance on the building, the roof had collapsed. There was four feet of water in the building's basement.

Goodyear was able to convince a court to award him an additional quarter-million dollars in damages.

Goodyear could not convince the court to help him find Hartman. That was my job.

On first look, it seemed a relatively straightforward assignment. We knew Hartman's address. The lawful judgment Goodyear had against Hartman gave us the power to restrain — or freeze — any monies of his we could find.

And that same judgment entitled us to legally access his credit report.

Do you know what your credit report looks like?

You should. It's the single most important record on you.

Contact each of the country's three credit bureaus (their reports can differ slightly) and get a copy of your report. You can order it by phone or download it directly over the Internet from Transunion, Experian (formerly TRW), and Equifax. (See "Protect Yourself" at the end of the chapter for complete contact information.)

These companies get their information from a variety of sources — including anyone who's granted you credit, as well as the public record documents we've been talking about.

If you've recently been denied credit, you're entitled to a free copy of your report as long as you request it within a specified time period. Otherwise, it will probably cost you a few bucks, depending on where you live.

When you get your report, make sure that there are no judgments or bills on it that aren't yours. If there are, straighten them out immediately.

You don't want someone else's civil judgment showing up on your credit record when you're trying to buy a house . . . which is what happened to my fellow writer when we were just starting this book.

PUBLIC RECORD, INC.

Want to get the lowdown on a particular company?

Run a D&B on them.

D&B stands for Dun & Bradstreet. In the same way credit bureaus and information agencies collect data on you, Dun & Bradstreet collects data on businesses. Some of that information comes from public records — federal bankruptcy filings, state corporate filings, local civil judgments such as liens, etc. Some comes from news sources — magazines, trade journals, and newspapers. And some comes from industry contacts.

A D&B report includes information like the company's name and address, its parent company's name and address, a dollars-and-cents summary of how much business it does, a list of its employees, and its net worth.

It'll also tell you the company's history, such as how long it's been around, any relevant stock data, and — most importantly, from my point of view — it'll give you details and background information on who owns the company.

One important thing to remember: Some of the information Dun & Bradstreet provides is given to it by the companies themselves — so it's not always the most objective data. D&B does send investigators out to verify much of that data, however.

Want to run a report on your ex-wife's marketing firm? Odds are Dun & Bradstreet has the information in its computers. Call at 800-234-DUNS — or visit them on the Internet at www.dnb.com.

Again, there are plenty of other companies who do the same kind of thing. Check our resources list at the back of the book.

Peter Hartman's credit report told me a number of interesting things about him.

He believed in living high on the hog. His credit card bills reflected a very lavish lifestyle. He had a number of unpaid debts — Goodyear wasn't the only one he owed money. And Hartman had plenty of money. More than enough to satisfy the judgments against him — each of which ran into hundreds of thousands of dollars.

Peter Hartman clearly believed it should be up to him to decide when to pay off his debts. Goodyear and I, of course, wanted to set up a more regular payment schedule. First, though, we had to find him.

Hartman's credit report also told me he had interests nation-wide — important clues that would lead to a real estate corporation in Florida, an insurance company in Las Vegas, a condo in Scottsdale, Arizona, and a second home in California.

I went to all of them, running stakeouts, diving in dumpsters, making friends with dozens of local law-enforcement personnel. I spent thousands of my client's dollars searching for Hartman. I ran his credit report — not once, but dozens of times. I ran his name through every public record database I could think of. I found no substantial trace of him.

Eight years passed.

I was on-line at the New York City clerk's office, searching through its databases on another matter. For some reason, Peter Hartman popped into my head, and just for the heck of it, I ran his name.

A new listing popped up.

A listing of a lawsuit that contained an affidavit of service. The normally careful Hartman had made a very big mistake: He didn't pay his lawyer's bill. His lawyer knew where he lived. His lawyer had served papers on him. That affidavit of service was public record — available for review, coincidentally enough, in the same city clerk's office where I was.

I went and got a copy. The affidavit listed — as I knew it would — the address the process server had gone to in order to serve Hartman.

A Bridgeport, Connecticut, address. Hartman's mansion.

I found Peter Hartman and his antique cars. Shortly thereafter, almost eight years after the courts awarded Paul Goodyear his money, it was finally sitting in his bank account.

❑ ❑ ❑ ❑ ❑

Your credit report is not supposed to be a public record, of course. It's supposed to be available only to those authorized to review your credit history (the rather lengthy list of those who can legitimately request a credit report is outlined in the Federal

Fair Credit Reporting Act, available on-line at **www.ftc.gov**).

But the reality is that anyone with a modicum of intelligence can get your credit report. If I have a girlfriend who works at the company that issued your credit card, she can get it. If I know a guy at a bank or a used-car company, he can run a report for me, too. Should those methods fail, obtaining back-door credit reports is now a multimillion-dollar industry onto itself. Your credit report lists those who access your credit history, but only for six months. And if someone is questioned about why he pulled your credit report, a bogus excuse involving a wrong digit of your social security number is usually sufficient.

Your credit header — that collection of data at the top of your credit report that lists name, year of birth, and social security number — is legally available to anyone, at any time, with no restrictions. It can sometimes include middle initial, complete date of birth, maiden name (if applicable), a list of all the addresses you've lived at, and current or last known employer.

To get that header (from one of the on-line databases, say), the only information I need is your name and an address — current or previous — which I can get by following you home.

So much for the protective legislation that exists.

WHAT COULD BE DONE

The records we've been talking about in this chapter — the ones kept on you by the government, the database firms, and the credit bureaus — are going to continue to be passed around by employers, individuals, and other organizations.

Part of the reason is economic. The government makes money — a lot of money — selling that information to the database firms. The database firms make money, in turn, selling that data to their customers — selling a list of people who hold fishing licenses to a sporting goods manufacturer, for instance.

Part of the reason is convenience. In the past, you couldn't walk into a department store and walk out with a new credit card. Now, the credit bureaus let potential creditors nationwide make informed decisions about your creditworthiness in a matter of minutes.

It's a system, however, with a lot of jagged edges at this point. How to smooth them out — to fix things so that your private information is better protected?

Any solution has to include real accountability: documentation — agencies should record (via photo ID when possible) to whom they give your information — and prompt notification — agencies must contact you when your information has been requested and/or given out.

We really don't have a choice. You can't undo the information that's out there. Big Brother has watched, and we're probably not going to be able to get him to stop watching now. (What he's seeing is way too interesting!) Similarly, we're probably not going to stop the flow of public information anytime soon. There is too much money involved. The simple solution, and the proper thing to do, is to provide a system of notification. If a person or government entity has the right to review certain information, surely the person whom that information is about has the right to be notified of an inquiry.

Our society did really well with the old-time public notices, usually posted in the village square. Surely, the technology exists to move proper "notice" from the tree in the town square to your computer screen or mailbox.

In the meantime, just know that to function in today's society, you're going to have a public record. The best you can hope to do is minimize the amount of information out there and misdirect those with less-than-honorable intentions who are looking for it.

How? Don't be so free giving out the address where you put your head down each night. Make it appear that you've moved. Use your lawyer's office, your accountant's address, a friend's address, or a mail drop. Or keep using an old address that's already out there, already filed. Don't give away your social security number, your home telephone, or your date of birth unless you're legally obligated to.

One final note regarding real estate-related records (transfers, deeds, mortgages, taxes, easements, liens, etc.). Man's home is his "castle," and a large target sign has been placed at its entrance for too long. The current availability of real estate-related records presents potential privacy problems for many people.

A very low-cost and uncomplicated Real Estate Privacy Trust System, administered by insurance companies, should be available to the everyday homeowner. The publicly listed owner would be the insurance company. True ownership would always be verifiable, but only through an added layer of privacy. Insurance companies would organize and guard this information with the same high level of security as they do life insurance-related data.

PROTECT YOURSELF

1. **Know the record-keeping laws of your local, county and state governments.** Simply telephone the various municipal offices and ask what information they collect and keep on file. Ask which records are available for public review. Ask what documents are considered confidential, why they're confidential, and under what legal authority they can be accessed. Some of the best investigators are local reporters because they know the ins and outs of reviewing public records. Suggest that your local newspaper, library, or civic organization make known all available local sources of public information.

2. **Check government public records for accuracy.** If you want to be completely safe, do this for every level of government — and every place you've lived.

3. **Think like an investigator, information specialist, or con man.** Or imagine you're an investigative reporter for a local television station. (They all use just about the same methods.) *You*, or that weird neighbor you've always wondered about, are the target of the investigation. How would you find out

everything there is to know about your target? (There is usually a paper trail that leads to any specific document. Most records don't just appear out of thin air. For example, a real estate tax lien will lead back to a property deed, which might lead back to a mortgage, but will surely lead back to a building permit or property deed transfer.)

4. Request a copy of your own credit history. Ask to be notified any time a creditor contacts a credit bureau in preparation for opening a new account in your name. Ask for an explanation of what everything on your credit report means. Make sure the information is right.

Transunion: 800-888-4213 or 800-916-8800
        www.transunion.com
Experian (formerly TRW): 800-682-7654 or 888-397-3742
        www.experian.com
Equifax: 800-685-1111 or 800-525-6285
        www.equifax.com

5. Learn from credit bureau fraud units. Consider them your friend. Get to know them and how they operate before you get ripped off. Call the credit bureaus and ask the fraud units for their advice on how to prevent credit fraud and what to expect if you become a victim. Ask them to send you a copy of their "tips in preventing credit fraud." Also, federal law provides that you are entitled to one free copy of your credit report (from each of the three national credit bureaus) during any twelve-month period if you believe you've been a victim of fraud.

6. Put your affairs in order. Take the death test. You are going to be dead in one week. Ask yourself what you want to clean up or get rid of. Certain items can be made very public in a probate court hearing.

7. Ask the people who know. Whenever you come across any type of public servant (cop, court clerk, file clerk, etc.) simply ask them: What type of databases do you have? Please tell me what files your office maintains? What information do you have on people and businesses, how do you access it, and is it available to the public?

8. Observe the flow of information when you obtain important documents. We've all lost or misplaced various types of documents: legal papers, permits, real estate documents, driver's licenses, auto registrations, transfer records, passports, various IDs. They were relatively easy to replace or duplicate, weren't they? Think about what paperwork was needed to obtain the records in the first place. All too often we're in a rush just to get the desired document and we don't watch the true exchange of information. Do you remember the contents of that passport application? What kind of information did you provide on your driver's license application? Take another look at forms you filled out years ago. You'll begin to fully understand how information spreads.

9. Borrow someone's identity. This is only make believe, of course. Just imagine how you would borrow someone else's identity. Then you will realize how easy it is for someone to borrow yours! Almost anyone can collect more documents about you than you probably have stored in your own personal files! Can that business card you left in the glass jar at Red Lobster hoping to win a free dinner give me enough information to borrow your identity? How would you borrow your secretary's existence to use while she's on a two-week vacation?

4

YOUR CAR

I SHOWERED WITH A DEAD MAN!

You expect the temperature to get cooler as you travel north — particularly if you're leaving the close confines of New York City for the leafy glens of upstate New York. But not on this particular July afternoon: It was the same sticky, sweaty, uncomfortable ninety degrees in the lot behind 1317 Portage Road as it had been in Times Square.

I parked the Mercury Sable I'd leased from Rent-a-Wreck between a filthy white sedan and an old Chevy Malibu with plastic wrap for a rear windshield (my car looked right at home there), peeled myself away from the hot seat, and climbed out.

I was looking a little run-down myself. The heat had added several large sweat stains to the rumpled clothes I was wearing. Add in the few days' worth of beard I'd neglected to shave, and I looked just like a guy who was very much down on his luck. Which, I reflected, is exactly how a man renting a room at the YMCA should look.

The Village People song to the contrary, it's not that much fun to stay at a YMCA. Through no fault of the organization, your typical Young Men's Christian Association boarder is not likely to come from the cream of society's crop — or if they do, he's definitely fallen a long way from that tree.

The Niagara Falls YMCA on Portage Road is typical of the organization's facilities: a tired, beaten, four-story brick building whose better days are long behind it. The desk clerk — a woman who, frankly, had seen better days as well, gave me a weary smile as I walked in and told her I wanted a room. She handed me a key for room 312.

I shook my head. "I'd like a room on the fourth floor, please."

The girl frowned. "The only room I have left on the fourth floor doesn't have a screen in the window."

"Is the air-conditioning working?"

She shook her head. "Sir, none of our rooms have air-conditioning. And without a screen, the bugs will eat you alive."

I took the fourth floor room anyway.

The accommodations were prison-cell quality (actually, I've seen nicer prison cells). My room had a wood-frame bed built out of two by fours, a desk that had apparently been chewed on by a mountain lion, and a chair that looked so fragile I never actually sat down on it.

The overhead lightbulb, at least, was very bright. And very popular, as the girl downstairs had warned me, with the local bug population.

I ignored them as best I could and walked to the window.

Leaning out and looking to my left, I saw a supermarket parking lot littered with garbage. To my right, there was a row of boarded-up houses. Across the street, the local hoodlums were standing around a telephone pole, waiting for something to happen.

I was waiting for something, too.

I was waiting for the dead man to show his face.

His name was Alvin Adler, and I knew that — official documentation to the contrary — he was very much alive, and in residence here at the Niagara Falls Y.

At one time Adler had been a bigwig on the eastern shore of Long Island — worth several million dollars. In his mid-sixties, he was a handsome, cultured, active, very intelligent man . . .

Who did a dumb thing. He got involved in a major case of fraud. The attorney on that case brought me in, and I'd been searching for Adler on and off ever since — all told, for about four years.

During that time, I'd followed Adler from Long Island to Norwalk, Connecticut, and then out to a post office box in Scottsdale, Arizona. You might say the trail went cold at that point. That's when a piece of mail I'd sent to his P.O. Box came back with the word "deceased" scrawled on it.

I might have stopped looking for Adler then, except for the memory of the many shenanigans he and his lawyer had pulled over the years. You never know, I told myself.

I kept his file in my list of active cases.

About a year later, I was running key names in those cases through public records — the records of the New York State Department of Motor Vehicles (DMV), to be exact — when I received a pleasant surprise.

Alvin Adler's name popped up.

It seemed that after surrendering his Arizona license, an Alvin Adler who'd given his address as 1317 Portage Road in Niagara Falls, New York, had received a New York State driver's license.

Was it the Alvin Adler I was looking for?

I couldn't be 100 percent sure from the information in the record — New York does not, like some other states, use your social security number as your driver's license number, or even list the social security number as part of the license information. But the date of birth was the same. This, of course, seemed like too big of a coincidence. Time to double-check and then check some more.

I dug a little deeper — again, using public records.

I called the tax assessor and the receiver of taxes in Niagara Falls and found out that 1317 Portage Road was owned by the YMCA. I telephoned the Y next and found that an Alvin Adler was staying there, in a fourth-floor room, with his own private phone. Did I want that number?

Indeed I did. But rather than call him myself (at this point, I didn't want to alert Adler — if indeed it was he — that someone was on his trail again), I had a girl phone. As she made the call, pretending to be looking for a guy named Tony, I listened in on the other line, along with Leo Kaiser, the attorney who hired me.

The second that Adler spoke, Leo nodded. We'd found our man.

I was on the road the next morning — and in bed, getting eaten alive by bugs, that night.

Whatever else you could say about the Niagara Falls YMCA, its tenants were certainly curious. Every time I opened my door the following day, every other door on the hallway — maybe a dozen all told — opened a crack as well.

I was curious too, of course. Every time someone went to the bathroom, I'd go, hoping to catch sight of Adler. Though I didn't know exactly what he looked like, I knew he was in his sixties. But everyone I'd seen was considerably younger.

I'd hoped to spot him coming or going from his room. But by early evening I realized my plan wasn't working. Later that night, I took a tour of the YMCA parking lot. There, I found a car that almost certainly belonged to Adler — reconfirming for me that we did have the right Adler and that he was still staying at the Y.

More on what helped me identify the car later.

I woke up the next day and decided to wash at least some of the grunge off my body before deciding on my next step. I slipped on the ratty old bathrobe I'd brought with me for the trip and headed down the hall to the shower.

As I turned on the water, I ran through a number of different scenarios in my head — none of which I was completely satisfied with. The problem was, Adler was a suspicious guy, and he'd been on the run for a long time. Any approach where I forced my way on him — such as knocking on his door or calling him up — ran the risk of scaring him off.

I reached for the soap . . .

And there he was.

Alvin Adler. Dead man. In all his six-decade-old, naked-flesh glory.

Before long, we'd struck up a conversation. I pretended I was a divorced father from Florida, looking to settle in the area — strongly implying that I might have some trouble with the law, maybe something to do with child support.

Adler smiled in sympathy.

"You know any good banks?" I asked. "I need someplace to put my money."

"Oh, yeah," he said. "I know the bank you want."

Forty-five minutes later, we were driving into town together, on our way to the Marine Midland Bank he'd recommended to me. "This is great," I told him as he dropped me off. We made vague noises about getting together that evening.

I made the not-too-farfetched guess that the bank he was so high on was, in fact, where he kept his own money. Seconds later I was on the phone to Leo in New York, who overnighted the necessary legal papers to freeze Adler's bank accounts.

I'd guessed right. Adler's assets were there and we were able to collect a portion of the money he owed my client.

The next day, Adler disappeared again.

His case is now back in my active file. Recently I ran a credit check on him (which we can legally do since we have a lawful judgment against him) and found out he currently owes the federal government $150,000.

Adler's one guy I'll keep searching for — probably even if his death certificate shows up.

❑ ❑ ❑ ❑ ❑

America's love affair with the automobile is almost a hundred years old.

To drivers everywhere — the newly licensed teen, the vacationing family, the retiring couple — a car has come to mean mobility, independence, romance, and adventure. Casting aside the fenced-in drudgery of the past for the limitless opportunity of the wide-open road. No ties. No boundaries. Nobody telling you what to do, when to get up, where to go.

In a single word, freedom.

Well . . . not exactly.

In exchange for the right to cruise Route 66 with the top down, you give up a certain degree of that freedom. The compact between you and the government grants you a license to drive — and grants them the information they need to make sure you don't abuse that privilege.

Pull out your driver's license and take a look.

All of the information you see there — and a whole lot more — is on file down at your local Department of Motor Vehicles. Information you provided when you applied for your driver's license.

Information now available to the public as part of your motor vehicle record — MVR, for short.

Different states call it different things — but virtually all of them are making money hand over fist selling this record to anybody who fills out the proper form and pays the required fee. Pay enough, and you're welcome to back your truck up to the DMV office and clean them out — figuratively speaking. Many states regularly sell their complete databases to information brokers. CD-ROMs containing, for example, Massachusetts and Wisconsin drivers' records, updated on a semiannual basis, are available from our old friends at Merlin Data.

What's in these records? Again, it varies from state to state. Your name and date of birth, for sure. Your driver's license number — another identifying tag to run through public records. In some states, the record includes your social security number.

New York State driving records — to Alvin Adler's detriment — include your address and date of birth. They also list any traffic convictions and accidents you've had over the last three years, and any alcohol- or drug-related convictions over the last ten years. Alabama (where your driver's license number *is* your social security number) provides five years' worth of moving violations in its records.

The Illinois Driver Services Department, to its credit, does not provide the driver's address in its records, and you'll wait ten days after your request before you receive any information. That's so the person of record can be notified of the name of the requesting individual. Most states do not have this notification requirement.

Remember Rebecca Schaeffer? A twenty-one-year-old actress living in California, who'd just had her first taste of success in a television show called *My Sister Sam*? She was murdered by a stalker who got her address from her MVR. A request she was never notified of.

I hate to bring this example up, because it's such an extreme one. But there are a whole lot of crazy people out there.

ROAD RAGE

Recently, a police officer friend of mine was off duty, driving north on Interstate 95 in Connecticut with his wife and children in a van he'd borrowed from his brother. Checking his rearview mirror, he suddenly saw a lunatic weaving in and out of traffic, changing lanes, going way too fast.

My friend doesn't want a confrontation — he's with his family. He moves over to the slow lane so the lunatic can pass. The lunatic — who planned on using that lane to pass my friend — nearly rear-ends him. Now the lunatic starts beeping his horn, screaming and yelling, and using all sorts of profane hand signals. Just the sort of thing you want to see with your kids on a Sunday afternoon drive.

Finally, the lunatic swerves past my friend and buzzes away.

But that's not the end of the story.

A week later, my friend gets a call from his brother — the registered owner of the van. The brother has just received a threatening letter in the mail. It's from the lunatic, who has translated his obscene hand signals into words.

The letter notes the date, time, and place of their "encounter," and goes on to warn that the next time they meet, the driver of the van just might wind up with his car in a ball of flames.

Understandably, the cop is concerned.

How did the lunatic trace the van back to my friend's brother?

Well, in addition to your driver's license information, each state DMV also keeps records relating to your car: ownership, registration, title, license plate number, and VIN (vehicle identification number, a unique seventeen-digit tag found in numerous locations on your car.) In this case, the lunatic provided the license plate number, and the Connecticut DMV supplied the rest.

Again, each state keeps track of different information — check with your DMV to see what their records contain.

This *very* public record (how much more visible can you get than a license plate number?) is one even the most experienced investigators sometimes overlook. Years ago, a case I was working called for extensive vehicular surveillance on some very dangerous people. We hired several private detectives to assist on the case, and as a precaution, ran a routine check of their license plate numbers.

Although they were among the most talented, experienced investigators in the Northeast — retired police officers and retired FBI agents — their license plates led to their home addresses . . . and their wives and children.

We certainly couldn't have our quarry finding out that information.

I immediately filed a DBA (Doing Business As) paperwork for a company called Harrington Associates in a distant county. Harrington then opened up a P.O. Box — and the investigators switched their vehicle registrations *and* their driver's licenses to that address.

This kind of thing may or may not be legal in your state. Find out. Get creative if you have to. Use a mail service (like Mailboxes, Etc.), a friend's house, or a relative's place of business for all your motor vehicle records.

If anything comes to that address for you, you'll know that

your state DMV's been fattening up its bottom line again by selling your personal information.

(You can apply this technique to some of the public records we mentioned in the last chapter, too. Try purchasing property under a different name — a DBA, for example, or a legal alias).

A MODEST PROPOSAL

Back to the lunatic and my friend, the cop.

Because a member of the law enforcement community was involved, no resources were spared in conducting a thorough inquiry as to where, and exactly when, the lunatic ran the van's license plate number through the DMV. But even with the full power of the law behind them, the best that investigators could come up with was that the plate information was requested through some big insurance company. Any one of several hundred people there could have accessed the records. Dead-end. No way to identify that lunatic . . .

Just as there's no way to identify any other road rager you come across during your daily commute, summer vacation, or trip downtown — those drivers who put your life at risk and then disappear down the road, leaving no clue to their identity.

Except, of course, for their license plate number.

Think about it. I know my friend the cop did after the lunatic shot past, but he was more concerned with acting as if nothing had happened for the sake of his children. Too bad. But what about the other drivers on the road? What if one of them had written down the pertinent information and sent it to the local police?

I submit that this particular lunatic's road rage might have been tempered had he seen the victim and witnessing vehicles writing down his license plate number.

New York State is among those trying to crack down on road ragers. State troopers have been out on the road for the past year in seven unmarked vans, each equipped with more than six thousand dollars' worth of video equipment. Thirteen unmarked patrol cars have just been similarly equipped.

Help keep your taxes down by pitching in.

Put a pen and paper within reach of your steering wheel. If we all did, I suspect it would result in a sizable drop in not only road rage, but other vehicular crime as well. That careless delivery truck driver would probably think twice about speeding off after sideswiping your parked car if he saw someone writing down his license plate number.

The next time you're out driving, try it out.

When you write, double-check the number and the state the plate is from. Write down other confirming characteristics: the rip in the vinyl top, whitewall tires, the dent in the side panel, the decals/bumper stickers, and any other identifying features. Describe the person in the car if you can.

If you don't want to risk writing while you drive, add a disposable camera to your glove compartment. Not only could it help identify road ragers, but if your car is damaged under any other circumstances, you also have an instant photographic record.

I'd go so far as to make this technique part of your driving test. After you're parked but before you get out of the car, the road test examiner should say, "You've just been sideswiped by that car — what are you going to do?" Now that's a defensive driving technique.

Here's another: If you don't have a pen and paper handy, let the road rager see you making a call on a cell phone. If you don't have a cell phone, just make believe. Hold your hand up to your ear and pretend you're calling 911.

And while we're at it . . .

There really should be a centralized telephone number that can take complaints from drivers who witness road rage. A letter of warning from the state police would make potential ragers think twice before going off the next time.

WHAT COULD BE DONE

There are fifty different laws regarding access to motor vehicle records. In theory, each of those laws provides protection for the private information you give up in exchange for the privilege of driving.

In practice, those laws are ineffectual.

Make a list of ten people you know. Without a doubt, one of them — a lawyer, an insurance company representative, a cop's kid brother, a legislator's wife — will be able to run a license plate for you.

If they can't, you can go out and hire a private investigator who'll do the job for you. It'll probably cost you fifty bucks.

This, by the way, is what Rebecca Schaeffer's killer did.

After that incident, California immediately tightened its laws regarding the release of motor vehicle records.

Of course, because of interstate reciprocity agreements — the same laws that allow you to drive in any state of the union — law enforcement personnel all across the country maintain the same level of access to those records. This, in effect, makes California's new vehicle records law useless.

The Federal Driver's Privacy Protection Act of 1994 attempted to address this problem.

The relevant subsection A of this law declares that state DMVs and their employees shall not "knowingly disclose or otherwise make available" motor vehicle records . . . except as provided in Subsection B.

Subsection A is one paragraph long and contains forty-eight words.

Subsection B lists the exceptions. It is nineteen paragraphs long, contains two additional layers of sub-subsections, and too damn many words for me to count.

Scheduled to go into effect in 1997, the Act was recently declared unconstitutional by two different federal courts on the grounds that it impermissibly regulated the state's control of its own property — motor vehicle records.

The federal government is appealing those decisions.

I contend that the law would have made little difference to anyone determined to access your motor vehicle records.

I submit there's more reason to be concerned about your driver's license and vehicle registration information than your credit cards. At least with your credit cards you get a monthly statement of activity. Who knows how many times your plate or driver's license has been run? The average citizen does not receive a driver's license and vehicle registration access activity report.

Any start at real reform in this area would include (again) documentation and notification.

How about national legislation that would notify you of the information request and subsequent release of any records pertaining to your vehicle registration or driver's license and require the individual requesting the information to be positively identified with a picture ID, for example?

SAY CHEESE

Oh, real quick, before I forget . . .

Take out your driver's license again. There's one very important piece of information on it we haven't talked about yet.

Your photograph.

I refer to it as information because on most state licenses, that's exactly what it is. A digital representation of your likeness, reducible to 0s and 1s in a computer — and thus, potentially available for purchase from your DMV.

THE MOST PUBLIC RECORD OF ALL

Let me take you back to that summer night in Niagara Falls . . .

The one where I'm walking through the parking lot of the YMCA, trying to find Alvin Adler's car.

If you remember my description of the part of town the Y was in, you know this wasn't exactly a nice place to visit. And the cars were pretty much what you'd expect to find in a parking lot of a place like that — old, beat-up, gas-guzzling dinosaurs. Except . . .

There was a very clean Ford Escort in the corner of the lot. Not a new car, not the kind of expensive car I might have expected former Long Island bigwig Alvin Adler to be driving, but by far the most reputable-looking car in this particular parking lot. I decided to check it out.

Up close, the Escort looked clean and well maintained.

I pulled out my flashlight and shone it inside the car.

I saw a couple of very fancy men's clothing catalogues on the passenger side seat — catalogues for people with a whole lot of disposable income. And on the shelf underneath the rear window, I saw a golf cap from an Arizona country club. Arizona — Adler's last known residence.

Adler's car? I would have bet money on it.

Sure enough, the next day, the undead dead man and I were riding in that Escort on our way to Marine Midland Bank.

❏ ❏ ❏ ❏ ❏

The easiest way for a person to get information about you from your car is . . . (drum roll) . . . by looking at your car.

I'm not talking about what the fact that you drive a Lexus or an Accord says about you. I'm talking about the bumper stickers on your car that tell the world what organizations you and your family belong to. And the parking decal that advertises where you live — and that you're not home.

And speaking of advertising —

How about that innocent-looking border around your license plate that proudly displays the name of the dealership where you bought your car?

"Hi, this is Harold from Joe Covo Matsura. You're enjoying the car? Good. Well, we're calling to offer you a free oil change and tune-up. . . . Yeah, that's right. Free. Okay, we'll be out tomorrow morning before noon to pick it up. . . . No, no — thank *you*."

Bye-bye new car.

Walk around your car and simply look at it. What identifying marks of any kind do you spot? Stickers that advertise where your kids go to school or the clubs you belong to?

A few phone calls and I'll determine what big events the school or the club has scheduled. I will then call you one week before to make sure you'll be attending the function . . . then I mark my calendar to attend the unadvertised garage sale you'll be holding that same evening.

Notice to all organizations: Parking stickers DO NOT have to identify your organization/facilities/individual members. Use symbols, numbers, or certain color schemes.

You don't see police officers putting police stickers on their vehicles, do you? Your bumper stickers should never provide assistance to the lunatics of the world. If you wouldn't walk up to the craziest person on the street and tell them you have a thirteen-year-old at the local school, you sure as heck shouldn't have a bumper sticker that reads: I'M THE PROUD PARENT OF AN HONOR ROLL STUDENT AT DEMPSEY HIGH SCHOOL.

And what advice would you give the very attractive young woman I saw driving through a nasty section of the Bronx with big signs in both her side windows advertising her car for sale — complete with telephone number! How about, "If you're after annoying phone calls, just write your phone number on the men's room wall at Grand Central next time!"

Be careful. Be alert. Be smart. Showing off your station wagon packed to the gills for a family vacation, with the kids reading comics in the back, is like begging someone to run the plate and go ransack your home.

PLAY DETECTIVE

Let's take a little trip for this exercise. Pick an afternoon when you've got some time, because this could take a while.

Our destination is the biggest parking lot near you — a Wal-Mart, a Home Depot, the Mall of America, etc.

Once you've got a location in mind, pick a color (decide before you go to the shopping center). Let's say you choose red.

When you get to the parking lot, find the nearest red car, and park as close to it as you can.

Now stop and examine that car.

What can you tell about the owner (leaving aside what they say about people who buy red cars)?

Start with what's visible from the outside of the car. Windshield decals, bumper stickers, inspection/official state notices. What shape is the car in?

Now look inside the car. What do you see?

Is the car a mess? Littered with Starbucks coffee cups? NRA literature?

Is there a magazine inside with a mailing label on it? A newspaper, a book, a program to a concert or cultural event?

I'll lay odds you will be able to get a pretty complete mental picture of the car's owner(s) from what you observe.

Now find out how close you were — wait until the people return.

Try not to stare at them too much, or you could end up explaining yourself to a cop — which is not the point of this exercise at all.

Were you right on? Try it again, if you like. Pick another color or just another car that looks interesting. Automobiles, like pet dogs, tend to look like their owners.

Or if you want some more practical applications . . .

Go check out your own car. Or one that belongs to your elderly relatives. See what you and yours are telling the casual passerby each time you pull into the grocery store parking lot.

PROTECT YOURSELF

1. **Become license-plate conscious.** Remember how easy it is to run a license plate these days. Have a pen and paper handy while you drive. Write down plate numbers when you see unusual things happening. Put a disposable camera (or small tape recorder) in your glove compartment. Make note of other descriptions: car make, color, distinguishing features, etc. You might be able to help the cops.

2. **Run your own license plate** the next time you're at the motor vehicle department. See what information is provided. Ask people you know if they know someone who can "run" a plate for you. See how easy it is to do.

3. **Use an alternate address** for your car registration or driver's license. Check your local laws to make sure this is legal.

4. **Conduct a vehicle privacy check.** Just walk around your car and observe. What do you see inside your car? Remove all printed matter that provides information you don't want to advertise. Be careful of bags or boxes with "expensive"-type logos. Keep an old sheet handy to throw over items in your car. Put other personal telltale items in the trunk.

5. **Remove stickers, decals, and parking permits** that can provide information about you, your work, or your private life from the outside of your car.

6. Think of the legal issues regarding your license plate. Ask yourself whether you should be notified that your license plate number is processed through a database. Ask yourself if your eighteen-year-old niece (or her parents) has the right to know that a man found her attractive and decided to "run" her plate to see where she might live or frequent? Do you believe you have the right to know if your vehicle was pulled over for speeding when your employee/friend/relative borrowed it?

5

YOUR TELEPHONE

ONE REALLY BAD BALD MAN

He is a practicing attorney who has been accused of stealing other lawyer's clients, threatened with jail time by numerous judges for disobeying their instructions, and reported to the bar association by court officials for abusing the legal system.

He has been sued for malpractice and has (allegedly) committed over a million dollars' worth of insurance fraud.

At one time he carried five different driver's licenses —from Ohio, New Jersey, Pennsylvania, and two from New York State (with two different dates of birth). Two license photos show him with a toupee. The other photos show him bald.

He has physically abused (sorry, he has allegedly abused) three of his ex-wives.

He owns a shotgun, a rifle, a .357 Magnum, and a .22 six-shot.

In short, he is a nasty, dangerous piece of work: the reason jail cells were invented. But no one seems able to put him there.

His actions have been totally out of control for a long time.

He's been called some unprintable names, but let's give him the name Benny.

I first encountered Benny several years ago when the attorney of his then-wife hired me to get her out of the mess her life had become.

Almost immediately, I developed an understanding of exactly how devious a character Benny was.

In the middle of his divorce proceedings, he began crying poverty, saying that any substantial child support payments would cripple him financially. And he produced papers in court attempting to substantiate the depth of his financial woes.

But something strange was going on.

I knew from "doing his trash" that he was spending lots of money. Through various receipts and billing statements that he'd discarded, as well as from surveillance operations, we knew he wasn't exactly subsisting on peanut-butter-and-jelly sandwiches. For one thing, he spent an awful lot of weekends flying to Miami.

Yet the bank records he produced in court showed a relatively modest (mid-five-figure) income.

The fog surrounding his financial situation began to clear one afternoon when we followed him to a car dealership in White Plains, New York. He spent close to an hour and a half inside.

I made the assumption that he was buying a new car.

I called the dealership the next day, pretending to be Benny's assistant. "I'm calling for my boss," I told the dealer. "He asked me to have you fax the car purchase information to his accountant."

A few minutes later, a copy of the bill of sale was faxed to the number I'd given the dealer for the "accountant" — which was, in fact, a nearby Mailboxes, Etc.

It seems that, in spite of his pleas of poverty, the lawyer had somehow come up with the money — cash — to buy a sixty-thousand-dollar Mercedes Benz. Of course, he was careful to have the car purchased through one of his corporate shells. Surely, we'd be seeing him behind the wheel of that new Mercedes in just a few short days.

At this point, I smelled blood. Given his patently false testimony in court, I thought we'd be able to nail him big time for appropriate child support.

But then, the car never showed up.

A week passed. Then another. And another. Benny goes about his business like nothing's wrong.

At which point I decided to check out what had happened. I headed down to the New York DMV . . . where I found no record of his owning a Mercedes Benz. There were no registration records under his name or under any of the various business names he'd been using. For some reason, that didn't surprise me.

Which is why I'd brought my copy of the car's bill of sale along. Because it included the Mercedes's VIN — the vehicle identification number, as you'll recall, that's part of the public record information the DMV keeps on every car.

Searching by VIN through DMV records, I discovered the Mercedes was registered to someone else — who (I verified shortly thereafter) was quite happily driving it.

What had happened? Benny, after buying the car through his sole proprietorship, had turned right around and sold it. He actually made a profit on the car since he had ordered it many months earlier and, not only had the sticker price increased, there was now a long waiting list of buyers. We found that he had advertised the new car for sale in the classified section of the *New York Times* and had already found a buyer before he had taken delivery of the vehicle.

He arranged to have his business buy the car with pre-tax dollars. Then the business used this "business vehicle" to write off expenses for another car — a BMW. So the taxman sees normal business expenses: insurance, repairs, gasoline, etc. Uncle Sam doesn't see that these expenses are really against a phantom automobile because Benny already sold the car. Of course, the payment for the Mercedes was made to Benny and not to the real owner of the car, Benny's company.

Devious, devious, devious.

It was a great scam.

But now we knew about it. Now we could go to the judge in the divorce case and show him that Benny wasn't anywhere near as destitute as he claimed.

One little problem:

We had to find the money first.

A task that I was quite sure Benny had made as difficult as possible — probably by putting the money into an account outside the United States.

Where?

I sat down with my clients and brainstormed.

After some discussion, we zeroed in on his weekend trips to Miami. The international airport there connected to hundreds of destinations worldwide. Maybe Florida was just a stopping point for him and his money. Surveillance hadn't revealed anything — we needed to know whom he was communicating with.

We needed his phone records.

Of course it's firm policy, which the telephone industry has observed since the days of Ma Bell, not to give those records out.

Notice I said policy — not law.

Your telephone records have no real legal protection.

Phone companies have bent their strict nondisclosure rule in the past for their own (commercial) purposes — such as when MCI went through all its long-distance records to identify "friends and family" of current customers who were using competing long-distance carriers.

ITT went MCI a step better by buying other companies' phone records and calling their customers to tell them how much they could save by switching to ITT.

Would it surprise you at this point if I said that on occasion, I've known telephone company employees to provide assistance in improperly obtaining customer phone records? It happened in the case of Benny and his wife, in fact.

Their court proceedings had been one of New York's most lengthy divorce cases ever. During this more than five-year period, Benny had always seemed particularly good at keeping track of his wife — and knowing all about the circle of friends she moved in.

We wondered how he was able to do this.

Then we found out Benny's brother worked at the phone company and regularly got him copies of his wife's telephone records.

Obtaining phone company records is a multimillion-dollar business, a method investigators use almost as often as public records. You can do it yourself. Run a search for "information brokers" on the Internet, flip through the classifieds of any daily legal newspaper (the *New York Law Journal*, etc.), or check the ads in the back of investigative journals. You'll find a hundred firms only too happy to help you.

Government investigators routinely go through phone records as a way of keeping track of "questionable" characters, such as organized crime figures. Not because they're looking for anything specific, but simply as a way of monitoring what that person's up to. If they see that Junior's making a lot of calls to a certain construction company in Freeport, then they might allocate a few agents to check the situation out further.

It's analogous to how the paparazzi stalk celebrities. They're not looking for anything in particular. They just go out there and snap away. Then they find a market for the dirt they dig up. A member of the paparazzi and a phone activity analyzer operate knowing that chances are good that something valuable will eventually appear.

❏ ❏ ❏ ❏ ❏

We didn't need anyone's help getting Benny's phone records. Because we were in the middle of a lawsuit with him, we simply subpoenaed them.

When those records arrived, one number stood out immediately. A long-distance call to Jamaica, repeated several times over the course of a month. We quickly found out that the number belonged to a fax machine . . . which belonged to one of the smaller banks on the island.

I was soon on my way to Jamaica. (Benny's story continues in Chapter 8.)

Your personal phone records are easy to exploit. But incredibly, there's another broad category of phone records that are even less secure than the ones listed on your home telephone bill — your employer's.

THE DAY THE MUSIC DIED:
THE WORKPLACE PHONE

In the days when AM radio ruled the airwaves, Rick Sklar was king. He was programming director of arguably the most powerful — and prominent — radio station in the country, New York's WABC, back in the 1960s and '70s.

On June 23, 1992, Sklar entered St. Luke's-Roosevelt Hospital in Manhattan for a minor operation. He needed a tendon in his left ankle repaired.

Sklar died on the operating-room table.

The anesthesiologist mistakenly inserted a tube intended to send oxygen to the lungs into Sklar's esophagus. The anesthesiologist also failed to note that the equipment intended to monitor the procedure wasn't working.

It was a tragedy.

The hospital quickly acknowledged its error, the anesthesiologist went on leave, Sklar's family initiated a lawsuit . . .

And information about the incident began appearing in the press. The details, which included Sklar's confidential medical records and hospital memos, were splashed across the front pages of several New York papers. The stories were embarrassing to the hospital and upsetting to Sklar's family.

Where was the leak? As the number of stories grew, it became clear that the only place the information could be coming from was a source inside St. Luke's.

Now St. Luke's-Roosevelt is one of the largest private hospitals in the United States. They have more than twelve hundred attending physicians, and close to five thousand nurses and support personnel on staff.

How in the world were hospital officials going to find out which one of those employees was leaking information on the Sklar case?

Actually, it was easy.

They simply consulted their phone records.

First, they identified the calls to the reporters, and the extension those calls were made from, which turned out to be the maintenance staff's lounge. Then, they cross-referenced the times of those calls against hospital maintenance duty rosters.

The guilty party turned out to be a maintenance man, intent on satisfying a grudge he had against the anesthesiologist by keeping the story of the Sklar tragedy at the top of the news.

He was promptly escorted out of St. Luke's.

❏ ❏ ❏ ❏ ❏

The courts have generally held that while on the job, you have the same right to privacy as any other hard-working zoo animal.

That is to say, none.

Keeping a detailed record of the phone calls made from your extension is one of the least intrusive acts the powers-that-be at your company are entitled to (they can go through your desk, your file cabinet, your computer, listen to your voicemail, install security cameras anywhere they deem necessary . . . you get the idea).

While you are at work, your business is your boss's business. You really don't have any personal privacy. Some people don't realize that those "quick, innocent" telephone calls to their grandmother in Italy are fully documented each month on a phone bill. People easily justify telephoning potential employers on company time as a common practice. But these same people are surprised, and possibly enraged and insulted, if presented with a telephone bill and a request for reimbursement.

You must become telecommunications-conscious — aware of what is involved in that apparent simple act of communicating. We were all told growing up, "Think before you speak." Today, we need to think before we dial. I suggest that we think about what we want to say *and* about the mechanics of the actual placement of the telephone call. Try it. It's very easy. As you prepare to dial a telephone number, think of how a record of that call is being made, where it will be documented, and who will have access to it.

WHAT COULD BE DONE

Should the private information the phone company collects about you and your habits have more legal protection?

I think so.

The phone company has a legitimate right to your name and address, the same way any creditor does. But the release of that information to third parties or the use of it for their own cross-marketing purposes should be subject to your notification and approval.

But the day has surely come that telephone bills don't have to reveal the numbers dialed. Or at least not the entire telephone number. Just as credit card companies give you a receipt with a number of the digits replaced with Xs, so too can the telephone companies on their billing records. For example, your telephone bill would show you dialed 202-223-XXXX. The same would hold true for cell phones. Some hotels have been following this practice for years.

There should be a federal law giving you this type of billing option. Essential to this law would be that telephone companies would have to program their processing and billing computers *not* to make a record of the full number, if you so desire. You would give up the chance to dispute minor billing errors, but again, that would be your option.

The complete record of all dialed telephone numbers could be maintained where the telephone is, in your home or office. That should be a possibility with the inexpensive units and the complicated pricing structure that exists today.

BEEP YOU!

On Fridays during the summer, New York City becomes a ghost town.

Everybody heads to the beach for the weekend, either out to the Hamptons in Long Island or down to the Jersey shore.

For some reason, I was still working that Friday afternoon in August when a call came in from Jack Douglas, a former FBI agent now working as a P.I. out of Dallas.

"Kevin," he began, "I need a favor."

"Shoot," I told him.

"I just got this big client — a socialite down here in Fort Worth — who thinks her boyfriend's cheating on her. He's a lawyer up in Westchester County, name of George Talley."

"Talley? The mob lawyer?"

"That's him," Jack said. "But this isn't mob-related. This is a strict surveillance job — I need somebody to tail him."

"When?"

"Now."

"Jack, you've got to be kidding. Everybody's down at the shore."

"Well, see what you can do. I'll pay you whatever you want," he said. "But it's gotta be tonight."

I hung up with Jack and made a bunch of calls.

I reached a bunch of answering machines. As I'd suspected, none of the investigators I usually used were around. I was able to talk to a couple of people, but they couldn't even get back to the city until the next day.

I called Jack back. "Best I can do," I told him, "is two guys for tomorrow morning."

"Gotta be tonight," he repeated. "Why don't you do it?"

"Jack . . . ," I began.

"It'll be fun," he said.

Silence.

"Kevin," he said. "This is very important to me. Please."

I took a deep breath, "What do you have, bubba? Talk to me."

The only information Jack had on Talley was his work address, his beeper number, and the fact that he drove a late-model BMW sedan.

I ran Talley's name through the DMV and picked up his plate number. Then I went out to his office on Central Avenue in White Plains — where I arrived just in time to pick up Talley pulling out for the day.

I don't know if he saw me pull out behind him or if he was just in a rush, but the first red light we came to — a fairly busy intersection in Westchester County — he gunned straight through.

I blasted through the light after him.

A few blocks later, he did the same thing. So did I.

Then he got on 684 North and really hit the gas.

When my speedometer hit ninety-five — and Talley was still pulling away — I'd had enough.

I pulled over and called Jack.

"Does your guy know somebody's onto him, or does he just drive fast?"

Jack laughed. "You lost him?"

"I didn't lose him," I said. "I just didn't feel like getting killed today."

I told Jack I'd check in with him tomorrow, because I fully expected to be back on Talley's tail by early morning.

The last comment Jack made to me was, "Reach into that bag of tricks and pull me out a good one, will ya?"

I checked into an area hotel and dialed Talley's beeper number.

For those half-dozen of you who may not know how beeper technology works, here's a brief rundown.

When I call your beeper number, I'm actually dialing in to a large company's telephone system. The number rings, and I then enter (on my touch-tone phone) the phone number I want the person to call, usually followed by the # key.

The satellite then transmits a signal to your beeper, which displays the number of the person who's just called you.

Beeper technology is getting ever more sophisticated. There

are models that can display text messages along with the number and some that can even download those messages to your hand-held organizer and personal computer.

When I dialed Talley's beeper number at nine o'clock that evening, he called me back at the number I'd given him right away.

Big mistake.

I hadn't had him dial the hotel where I was staying. Instead, I had him dial an associate I'd managed to reach in the meantime.

We were able to see that Talley was calling us from a number in the 914 area code — Westchester County, New York.

My associate let the phone ring until Talley got tired of calling. Then we ran the number through a reverse directory, which lists phone numbers in numerical order followed by the name and address.

Surprise: It came back to a woman. It looked like Talley's Texas girlfriend had been right to suspect him of stepping out on her.

My next step was to call back the two guys who told me they'd be free for a tailing job starting Saturday morning. I gave them Talley's description and told them what kind of car he drove and where he would be the next morning. I wanted details on Talley and the woman he was seeing, what they did, where they went, etc.

Then I took the woman's name and started running it through some databases. It turned out she was a lawyer with a firm that shared his office building.

I took a break to grab a few hours of sleep — and was woken up at 7 A.M. by a call from one of the guys on the tailing job.

"We lost him."

"What happened?"

"About half an hour ago, the lights go on inside the house. We see your guy and this woman kiss goodbye, and he comes out and climbs into his car. And then he takes off — I mean, he's doing seventy in a thirty-five-mile-an-hour zone. He blows past a couple stop signs, gets on the highway, and guns it — he had to be goin' at least a hundred — and then he disappears."

"Lovely," I said. "Check back with me in a few hours — I may want you to pick him up again."

I reported in to Jack.

"Stay on him," he said. "My client wants details."

I laughed. "Stay on him! You've got to be kidding. We've only been able to stay on him for a total of four minutes. Thankfully he's falling for the beeper trick. We'll try it again tonight."

So we did. This time, I arranged for another associate — a woman — to receive Talley's call. She answered and told him he had a wrong number.

Then she called me and gave me the number Talley had called from. A 203 number, somewhere in Connecticut.

I called friends in Connecticut. They traced that number back to another woman who lived in a very nice part of Westport. I gave her address to the guys working surveillance for me and ran her name through a few databases.

Surprise, surprise: Talley was spending his Saturday night with his ex-wife.

I filled Jack in on this latest development. Then I went and joined my guys on the stakeout.

Sunday morning rolled around and — just like the day before — Talley got up early, kissed his ex-wife goodbye, and hopped into his BMW.

We stayed with him a little longer this time — only because it was Sunday, I guess, or because he was on his way to his mother's for lunch. But once he hit the highway after lunch, he was gone again.

We did the beeper trick Sunday night around 8 P.M.

This time, Talley called us back from a Bedford, New York, address. Which turned out to be a property that he actually owned . . . where he lived with his wife.

"You're not gonna believe this," I told Jack when I got on the phone with him.

Neither did his client.

She was on a Monday morning flight into La Guardia and at Talley's office by noon.

Theirs was not a happy reunion.

❑ ❑ ❑ ❑ ❑

The government is quite proud that "only" a thousand or so "legal" wiretaps are approved each year. Don't let that statistic fool you. They're not counting the hundreds of thousands of concerned spouses, parents, girlfriends, boyfriends, and businesspeople who listen to and record conversations in violation of the law. The average person who illegally wiretaps views this act with the same seriousness as driving two miles an hour over the speed limit. Also, this act is usually committed by a person who's not thinking clearly, in the throes of a highly emotionally charged situation, frantically only wishing to "know the truth."

Short of investing thousands of dollars in signal-scrambling equipment, there's really no sure way to guarantee the phone call you're making is completely secure.

You have to assume that your cellular and cordless conversations are not private, and converse accordingly.

❑ ❑ ❑ ❑ ❑

There's no harm in letting someone know where you're calling from. Unless it's someone trying to figure out if you're home or not. At work or not. Where you said you'd be. Where you're supposed to be.

Play it safe.

If somebody beeps you and you don't recognize the callback number, consider just not calling the number back. What if it's a friend? Use a pre-arranged code — say 333 — at the end of the number, so you know who is calling you. Or friends can have codes that correspond to their initials.

THE BOOK OF THE FILM

No one tells this story better than the friend of mine who asked me to assist him on this case. Once you've heard it, you can join me in telling him to write it down and sell it to the movies. I've already cast the film in my head: Jon Lovitz is the husband, Carmen Electra his wife, Matt Damon the fireman, and as my friend — the investigator the husband hires — Gene Hackman. I don't know about Hackman but my friend views my suggestion as a compliment.

Just to keep things simple, I'll refer to the characters in this story not by their real names, but by the actors who will play them in the movie — Jon, Carmen, Matt, and Gene.

Jon is a hard-working hot-dog vendor in Westchester County (just outside New York City) convinced he's destined for better things in life. His beautiful wife Carmen used to believe the same thing — but over the last few years, has begun to feel she's made a mistake in tying herself down to Jon. She's become a workout freak, who spends more time at the gym and hanging out in bars with her girlfriends than with Jon or the children. Jon is starting to suspect that Carmen is stepping out on him — and he's hired my friend Gene to shadow her.

One afternoon, Gene follows Carmen from her workout class to a bar, where she meets one of her best girlfriends. The two spend a couple of hours there, socializing, drinking, laughing — harmless, innocent, girlfriend kind of fun.

I had been able to start talking to the women and bought them a few rounds of drinks. We were starting to have a real good time when, all of a sudden, I am quickly ignored, dropped, and dismissed. (Ouch!)

The firemen had arrived.

Whether they've just gotten off shift from a nearby firehouse, or they've arranged to meet at the bar, Gene doesn't know. But the six smiling, strapping young men who walk in — led by Matt Damon — are clearly there to have a good time.

Very shortly, Carmen and Matt are doing just that — first at the bar and later at a hotel adjacent to the Whitestone Bridge outside of Manhattan.

That evening, Gene has the unhappy task of informing Jon that his suspicions appear to be well founded. He provides what details he can. Jon goes ballistic.

He wants to find Matt and punch his lights out. He wants to find Carmen and punch her lights out. He wants an apology. He wants her dead.

He wants Gene to follow her again.

Only this time, he wants the whole story — details included. And he's willing to pay my friend — I mean, Gene — big money to get it.

Gene agrees. He's noticed that Carmen is practically grafted to her cell phone. Which, given the equipment Gene's got, makes her calls as easy to monitor as if she were broadcasting them from the top of the Empire State Building.

So the next day, Gene parks his van a few houses down from Jon and Carmen's. When she leaves to go to the gym, he pulls out behind her.

She's on the phone almost before she's out of the driveway.

He's listening in as she begins calling every fire station in Queens, looking for a fireman named Matt. There's no possibility of getting the wrong guy — Carmen's description ("Six feet two inches, about 210 pounds, sandy blond hair, bright blue eyes, muscular — but not too muscular") doesn't leave much room for error. Still, there are a lot of firehouses in Queens — she doesn't find her man until much later in the afternoon.

When she does, it's a bit of an awkward reunion.

"Matt. It's Carmen."

"Oh." There's a pause on the line.

"Aren't you glad to hear from me?"

"Sure I'm glad to hear from you . . . but, uhhh, Carmen, how did you find me?"

She tells him.

"Hey, Carmen — that was a one-night thing we had, you know? Just some fun, right? We talked about that." Matt sounds a little nervous.

She laughs. "Hey listen, sport. I don't want a relationship with you either. I just want to get together with you a couple times a week and have sex."

"Oh." Now Matt is laughing. "That's cool."

The two spend the next few minutes talking about what kind of sex they want to have. Write the scene yourself.

That night, Gene gives Jon a tape he's made of Carmen's calls. Gene says, "It's a long tape, almost two hours total. Boy, can she talk!"

But because it's so late in the evening when the two men hook up, Jon goes to bed thinking he'll get up early and listen to the tape. He can't sleep, he's tossing and turning. He gets up and goes down to the kitchen. As he's putting the earphones over his head, Carmen walks in. "Are you okay, honey?" Jon can barely look at her. They eventually go back to bed. Jon spent the whole night staring at the ceiling and seeing how high his blood pressure could rise.

So the next morning, on his way to pick up hot dogs and fresh buns, he gets pulled over by a cop for driving erratically. Jon was so angry listening to the tape he could barely see, let alone drive straight. Gene, being the understanding guy he is, goes to the hot-dog stand that morning to see how Jon is doing. There's Jon wearing his Walkman, in an animated rage, stabbing hot dogs, flinging onions everywhere and yelling at just about every customer. Gene keeps walking and decides to have a slice of pizza for lunch.

My friend never tires of telling me this story — especially when he gets to imitate Jon simultaneously piling on the sauerkraut and cursing out Carmen.

❑ ❑ ❑ ❑ ❑

You probably aren't surprised that it's easy to monitor cellular phone calls.

You may have been on a cell phone yourself and heard another conversation just float by. Maybe it even contained some juicy stuff. This happens by accident. Imagine the kind of eavesdropping that can be done with just a little effort.

Wait — you don't have to imagine it. Go out and pick up a copy of *Spaceworm, I Listen* (published by Incommunicado Press).

This book contains transcripts of actual cellular conversations from around the country. The author monitored calls using commonly available, inexpensive equipment without the consent, without even the knowledge of the conversing parties.

A couple of years ago, you could go down to your local Radio Shack and pick up a scanner that would let you monitor cellular calls. It's more difficult now. Now, the over-the-counter scanner needs to be slightly modified. Basic enhancements anyone with limited electronic experience can accomplish in minutes. You may be able to find a used enhanced scanner at a pawnshop, tag sale, or a used electronics store. It's worth picking one up and bringing it home.

Because while monitoring cellular phone calls is illegal, monitoring calls made using a cordless phone is not. And once you see how easy it is to pick up cordless phone calls, I think you'll be a lot less free with the kind of information you give out over your home cordless phone. Demonstrate how complete a lack of privacy your cordless calls have to your teenage children as well. I guarantee you'll see a dramatic drop in your phone bill.

Here's a good way to think about every cellular and cordless telephone conversation you make: Just visualize a word balloon over your head, displaying every word you speak.

THE REDIAL BUTTON

It's everywhere these days, on every type of phone — cordless, cellular, land-line, even on your fax machine. The redial is a nosy person's best friend. It's also a terrific tool for investigators.

I recall one situation where a woman came to me because her brother had disappeared, leaving no clue to his whereabouts. The family was Polish, and it turned out that the father had faked the identification papers necessary to get them into the country twenty years earlier. The brother had been working in a hospital while studying to be an RN. He was a month or two short of getting his diploma when the hospital personnel department advised him that not only was he using someone else's social security number, he wasn't even a U.S. citizen. Furious when this information was revealed, the brother cut off all contact with his family.

They'd last heard from him a year earlier. He simply disappeared.

"What happened to all his belongings?" I asked the father.

He told me he had them up in his attic. There wasn't much — a battered typewriter, some clothes, books . . . and an old combination phone/answering machine. With a redial button.

I plugged in the machine and hit redial.

I reached Johnny's Airport Taxi — a Long Island company that only serviced JFK and La Guardia airports in New York. They confirmed they'd taken the son to Kennedy on the night in question. But he hadn't run off.

He'd been deported — back to Poland.

When the brother had become old enough to work, his father had just made up a social security number. Sadly, it was only when this tax-paying, hard-working young man had filed to take his RN exam that the truth was uncovered.

The redial button can be an investigator's best friend.

It could also be your worst nightmare.

Are you thinking about leaving your job? Was your last call before stepping out for lunch to a potential new employer?

Are you thinking about leaving your abusive husband/wife? Did you just hang up with the true love of your life?

Be careful. If you have a concern, erase the redial memory.

Wait for a dial tone, press one button on the phone keypad,

and hang up.

PLAY DETECTIVE

Good morning, Mr./Ms. Phelps.

Your assignment — should you choose to accept it — is to assemble a dossier on one of your coworkers, using only his or her telephone conversations as a source of information.

We strongly suggest you profile the coworker who sits nearest your office/cubicle/workstation, in order to arouse the least suspicion possible. The coworker chosen should be one with whom you have a strong friendship.

This assignment is to be completed surreptitiously. On the average, the dossier we seek can be assembled from one week's worth of phone calls.

Our goal is to assess the degree to which the average person consciously or unconsciously reveals personal/private/potentially hazardous information about himself during the course of the workday.

We suggest you conduct your assignment in the following manner.

Begin by setting aside a specified period of time each day to monitor your target. Monday mornings are often informative, as they are utilized by the average coworker to recount the weekend's adventures.

Purchase a stenographer's notebook, or obtain a spare one from the office supply closet. Use this notebook to keep a record of each call your target makes. Note the information discussed, as well as the time and date of each conversation.

At the end of each day, write a one-paragraph summary of what you've learned about your target.

Do not expect instant results. The possibility exists that your target will not reveal substantive amounts of information during many of the phone calls. Ignore the temptation to get back to work, and concentrate on the task at hand.

Only you can be the judge of when your assignment is complete. Resist the urge to comment on quantity of repetition and useless banter.

At that time, present a copy of your findings to your coworker.

Then ask your coworker to do the same to you. It's fine that you're now forewarned; your coworker will welcome the opportunity anyway. You will have a good lesson in being conscious and careful of what you say on the telephone.

As always, should you be caught, the authors of this book will disavow any knowledge of your mission.

Good luck.

PROTECT YOURSELF

1. **Assume someone is listening to your telephone conversations.** Assume that your cellular calls are either being recorded or have just floated into another nearby cellular conversation. Assume a neighbor's receiver of some kind (baby monitor, cordless telephone, intercom, etc.) is inadvertently broadcasting your cordless phone conversation. If you have heightened privacy concerns, assume that your land-line telephones (phones with actual wires: pay phones, home and work telephones) are tapped into and your conversations are being monitored.

2. **Become telecommunications-conscious.** Think before you dial. Say to yourself, "There will be a record of this phone call." This includes all telephone calls from work and home, dialed fax numbers, beeper numbers you dial, and calls placed to cellular phones. Someone will have access to the documentation that the call was made: a marketer, a salesman, reporters, nosy people, an adversary, etc.

3. **Perform a "privacy test" around your house.** Pick up a used scanner and see how public your private conversations really are. Have someone place a telephone call on your cordless

telephone. Then put your scanner in "seek" mode and see what happens.

4. Get into the habit of clearing your phone's redial memory. After you hang up, pick up the phone, wait for a dial tone, press one button on the phone keypad, and hang up.

5. Use random pay phones for your most sensitive calls. This, of course, is an extreme measure but one you, a friend, or relative might have to resort to if you're in an emotionally charged situation involving violence, for instance. Take no chances when complete privacy is essential.

6. Use a disposable telephone charge card for your long-distance calls. You see them everywhere now, at gas stations, delis, etc. Buy an inexpensive one and see how they work. Carry one with you just in case. You just might not want certain telephone numbers appearing on your work or home telephone bill.

7. Know what telephone technology is available in your area. Call your local telephone company and ask for information regarding features like "call return," "call blocking," "caller ID," etc. Ask, "What features do you have that can help protect my privacy?" New technology is constantly coming out. Read the small advertisements that come with your bill. Weigh the advantages (to your privacy, etc.) against the disadvantages (usually cost).

8. Don't be too anxious to return calls to an unfamiliar number displayed on your beeper. Do you call back numbers you don't recognize when you are beeped? Be careful. Arrange easy-to-remember codes. For example, 22 (BB) following a number can mean it's a member of your baseball team; 911 means it's an emergency. Your friend with the initials J.V. could always enter "58" after the number he beeps you to.

9. Check all physical telephone wires. If you have privacy concerns, walk around your home and work and identify the telephone wires. Can they be easily compromised? Can someone just hook right into them? Consider having your telephone wires enclosed in conduit like electrical wires. (I strongly maintain there could be more of a shock from telephone wires — and the subsequent eavesdropping — than the jolt from electrical wires.)

10. Think before you dial an 800 number. Once you do, you will become part of a detailed list that could show up in marketing databases around the world.

YOUR MAIL

DOUGIE DOES PARIS

Fifty-seventh Street in Manhattan has always been one of the most prestigious shopping addresses in America. High-end retailers like Chanel, Bergdorf-Goodman, Bendel's, Laura Ashley, and Burberry have made the street a favored destination of the hip, young, fashion-conscious consumer to whom money is no object. The beautiful people, in other words.

The gentleman I was watching walk out of Hermes, shopping bag in hand, was not a beautiful person. At five foot ten, 250 pounds, in his blue jeans and sweatshirt, he was neither hip, young, or fashion-conscious.

But Doug Arena — Dougie, as we liked to call him — did have a helluva lot of money. And he was spending a nice big chunk of it that day on Fifty-seventh Street.

"This guy's gonna have to stop and buy a new car to carry all the crap he's getting."

I turned to Charlie, the sharp, retired NYPD detective who was assisting me on the case, and nodded. Charlie and I had spent the better part of this sunny July day walking up and down Fifty-seventh Street watching Dougie spend his money. Actually, it wasn't really his money. A big chunk of it belonged to the people who'd hired us.

Dougie, you see, was a con artist, a Brooklyn boy made good, a "real estate developer" who'd started out renting apartments in Queens and ended up with a mansion on Long Island's northern shore. Along the way, he'd bilked dozens of investors out of a couple million dollars. One of those investors had hired me.

We'd been able to get a judgment against Dougie — but we were having a hard time tracking down his money. Public records revealed that Dougie had set up literally dozens of different corporations in New York, New Jersey, and Connecticut — and that apparently several other cases of alleged fraud were pending against him as well.

Dougie was smart, though. Every car he drove, every phone and credit card he used came back to a corporation. The only way we could find out where he lived was through his wife's motor vehicle record.

Once we had his address, Charlie and I stuck to him like glue for over a week. We went to his dentist, we found out where he liked to buy his coffee in the morning, what his favorite restaurants were. But we could find no trace of where he was hiding his money.

Today looked like another dead-end day of surveillance.

"Hey, hold on," Charlie said.

I looked up.

Ahead of us, at the corner of Fifty-seventh Street and Park Avenue, Dougie was walking into a Citibank.

We crossed the street. I stood next to Charlie while he pretended to make a call at a pay phone. Inside the bank, I saw Dougie walk over to a counter and fill out several slips.

"Here he goes," I said. "He's getting in line."

Dougie reached a teller and handed her the slips. Then he waited.

The teller looked over the slips. Then she picked up the phone and made a call.

Dougie leaned over the counter and said something. She smiled.

"This sleaze is hitting on the teller," I told Charlie.

She hung up the phone and wrote something down.

Then she reached into a drawer, pulled out a handful of cash big enough to choke a horse, and handed it over to Dougie.

"Bingo," I said. "We got him."

The next morning we handed the manager of that Citibank branch a restraining order commanding them to freeze Dougie's bank account to pay off the judgment we had against him. An accompanying subpoena instructed them to reveal how much of Dougie's money they had on deposit and to provide other potentially useful information.

An hour later, Citibank came back with their answer.

They had none of Dougie Arena's money on deposit. In fact, they didn't have anyone under that name banking with them.

We gave them Dougie's social security number and told them to cross-reference that against their accounts.

Nothing.

A list of his corporate names. Nope.

Dougie simply wasn't a customer of theirs.

So what had he been doing in that branch?

Surveillance wasn't getting us the information we needed. So Charlie and I decided to try a different approach. We paid a visit to Dougie's Glen Cove mansion.

Glen Cove (located on Long Island's northern shore) is a town where your social status is directly proportional to the size of your household staff. Dougie, despite all his millions, wasn't that high up in the social register. He had only one live-in maid and a part-time gardener.

Our hope was to find a time when the man and woman of the house were away and pump one of the help for information.

The next day, we drove out to Glen Cove, arriving at Dougie's mansion shortly after noon. There were no cars in the driveway.

"Maybe we got lucky our first time out," Charlie said as we climbed out of the car. There was a long winding path that led from the driveway around to the front of the house. As we were walking down it, we met the mailman going the other way.

He tipped his hat to us.

"Good afternoon," he said.

I grunted something in response as we continued on towards the house.

Dougie's mansion had a screened-in front porch, with a mail slot in the screen door. As Charlie and I stepped inside the porch to ring the doorbell, we couldn't help but notice the mail the postman had delivered, scattered across the floor. Several envelopes were visible, but one in particular caught my eye. It had the distinctive Citibank logo in the upper left-hand corner and a very unusual return address.

Charlie was about to ring the doorbell when I grabbed his arm and pointed to the ground. A split-second later, he caught sight of the envelope and the return address on it. His eyes lit up.

The envelope was addressed to Douglas Arena in Glen Cove. No pseudonym, no corporate shell. It looked like a bank statement.

It was from Paris, France.

That afternoon, we initiated a series of phone calls that led us from Dougie's Paris account to a number of shell corporations in Florida. We discovered Dougie was funneling his money overseas and having it wired back to New York as necessary.

Within a few weeks, we were able to get our clients a significant portion of their money back. And all because of a casual glimpse at Dougie's mail.

Kind of makes me wish I'd been a little friendlier towards that postman.

❑   ❑   ❑   ❑   ❑

As your mail makes its way across the office, across town, across the country, at virtually every step of the way it is susceptible to being compromised. I don't mean that your letters are steamed opened and the contents read (though I do know of a compound you can use that, when sprayed on an envelope, will render it transparent for thirty seconds). I don't mean compromised in the sense that your copy of *Sports Illustrated*'s swimsuit issue may have been passed around by a few postal workers or mailroom employees before continuing on its way to you.

I'm talking about compromised in the sense that someone has observed and taken note of valuable information about you from what you receive in the mail. Everyone who sees your mail can potentially turn certain information around and use it against you, the way I used it against Dougie. For example . . .

The uniquely shaped envelope from a travel agency lying on your kitchen counter tells the refrigerator repairman's assistant you're going on vacation. Your trip might be a nice opportunity for him to get back into the breaking-and-entering business.

The newsletter from the Kiwanis Club tells him you're likely to be out of the house the night of their annual awards ceremony. The mail-order computer catalogs, the *Popular Science* magazine, and that CD-shaped package from BMG Music Service with your monthly selection enclosed tells him you love electronic toys — and probably have a nice collection somewhere in the house.

I am amazed that credit card companies will discreetly mail your credit cards but then boldly blast their logo on other mailings, including statements. I don't necessarily have to see a bank statement to know where you bank. A simple piece of junk mail with the Union Bank logo will work just as well.

A cursory look at your mail can also provide a good con artist with the opening gambit they need to get you to lower your guard, perhaps in a casual conversation or in a bogus sales call. Information about your habits and your hobbies can be a potential bonanza for con men and privacy invaders.

"Hey . . . *Popular Mechanics*. I get that magazine. Did you do the project last month? Yeah? I couldn't get that to work. Maybe I could come over and look at what you did. . . . How about the weekend? Oh? You're not around? Well, how about during the week — what nights are good for you?"

And before you know it, you've just blurted out your social calendar for the entire year.

What can you do to protect yourself?

A good first step is to make sure your mail is delivered into a locked environment. That is, not to the old-style flag mailbox out on your street, not through a slot through which someone can peek, but into your house or a box only you can access.

Remember to be alert when you're going to have strangers in the house — repairmen, utility workers, etc. What telltale items (not just mail, for that matter) are you leaving out for them to get a close look at?

Mail stacked up outside your door or overflowing your mailbox is a telltale sign that you're on vacation. Have a friend come over and pick up your mail. Filing a stop mail order is probably not a good idea — the really clever crooks will actually be watching your neighborhood for the stops the postman doesn't make.

Unfortunately, it's not just con artists you have to worry about. After all, the post office is run by human beings. For every thousand trustworthy employees, count on a bad seed popping up somewhere. . . .

LISTEN TO WHAT THE (FAT) MAN SAID

Seinfeld reruns are one of the most watched shows on television these days. A fact I'm sure the post office would rather not be true. One of the show's most popular characters is Newman, Jerry's overweight, unfriendly, dishonest neighbor . . . who happens to be a postman.

A postman who tells his girlfriend zip codes are meaningless.

Who "borrows" a mail delivery truck to transport a shipment of empty five-cent bottles to Michigan, where they'd be worth a dime.

Who complains that the mail never stops: "Every day it piles up more and more and more and you gotta get it out. But the more you get out, the more it keeps coming in. And then the barcode reader breaks!"

Not the calm, in-control image the U.S. Post Office would like to present to America.

Still, Newman has his moments of insight. One in particular

struck me a few weeks back. I was channel-surfing in a Red Roof Inn, killing a few minutes before I had to go out on a trash run, when I came across *Seinfeld*.

Newman and Kramer were sitting in a restaurant, when in the middle of a discussion, Newman leans over the table and says to Kramer in a conspiratorial whisper:

"Whoever controls the mail controls information."

The U.S. Postal Service does control your mail — and some very personal information about you. Specifically, your name and address . . .

Which, once you fill out the post office's official change of address form, they provide to anyone who pays to subscribe to the National Change of Address (NCOA) system. Subscribers include the credit bureaus, direct mail companies, and government agencies.

They keep that change of address card on file at your old post office. A few years back, anyone could walk into that post office, fill out a form and get a copy of it. Today your information is supposed to be available only to law enforcement personnel or those trying to serve you legal papers.

So, any person interested in your address must now create the circumstances (or legal papers) the post office requires. It's illegal, but it's easy and it's done all the time.

There's a process server in Baltimore, Maryland, who routinely travels around with blank subpoenas and unrelated lawsuit papers so he can present bogus documentation to post office clerks who simply don't understand the legal papers in front of them.

I can also find your new location by sending an empty envelope to your old address and paying a nominal fee for a service called Address Correction Requested. You've seen those three little words written on a lot of your mail, I'm sure. All they mean is that instead of forwarding the mail to you, the post office will return it to me with your new address written on it.

What else does the post office do with your name and address information?

Perhaps you've seen that other famous television postman,

Cliff from *Cheers*, hawking a line of Pitney-Bowes products. Prominently featured is "your personal post office" — a computerized postal meter machine that you can use for your small business's mail. In a brilliant stroke of cross-marketing, they're also offering a CD containing a list of customer names on it so you can begin your mailings.

Who are those customers?

You guessed it: anyone who's filled out a change-of-address card in the last few months, plus hapless hordes of people on other mailing lists.

❑ ❑ ❑ ❑ ❑

Most of us aren't likely to think of the post office when we imagine the modern, high-tech corporation. Even though we know about its automated zip code readers and the computerized Express Mail tracking system, when you think about the typical postal worker you're likely to visualize your friendly neighborhood postman, walking her or his route with an old-fashioned mail sack. Or the helpful post office clerk, selling stamps and money orders.

Or — again to the dismay of the Postmaster General — Newman.

Odds are, you don't think about the highly trained force of nearly twenty-five hundred armed federal officers, backed up by state-of-the-art forensic laboratories, specialized technical inquiry sections (including experts on fingerprints, documents, chemicals, and digital analysis), and the authority to intercept and log every piece of your incoming and outgoing mail.

These officers are responsible for over twenty-six thousand arrests over the last five years, played a key role in such high-profile cases as Michael Milken and E. F. Hutton, and annually help recover over $50 million in counterfeit postage stamps.

America's secret army: the Postal Inspectors.

THE LAW'S LONGEST ARM

He was taking a shower.

She was pacing back and forth in the hall, waiting for the mailman.

It could have been a slice-of-life from any married couple's daily routine. They'd certainly set it up to look that way.

The house in the Hollywood hills, the BMW in the driveway, the vase of yellow roses sitting on the kitchen counter — all the details smacked of a normal suburban existence.

It was all a sham.

The flowers (visible to anyone opening the front door) were there for show only.

The BMW had been rented using a forged driver's license and a stolen credit card.

And it wasn't even their house.

Posing as a married couple (they were, in fact, brother and sister), the man and woman had a local real estate agent show them the house earlier in the week. While the sister and the agent talked about how wonderful it would be to remodel the kitchen the right way, the brother was unlatching a window in one of the downstairs bathrooms.

They returned two days later to receive the Priority Mail package they'd arranged to be delivered to their "new" address. There was absolutely nothing tying them to the house. They'd given the real estate agent a false name as well.

Doris and John planned to take delivery of their package, lock the door (and the bathroom window), and walk out of the house without anyone knowing they were ever there. Let the various Realtors showing the house wonder who left the flowers.

They were in for a rude awakening.

In the wooded hills surrounding the house, half a dozen Postal Inspectors (as well as a dozen other federal and local law enforcement officers) were waiting, ready to arrest Doris and John Poole on charges of forgery, conspiracy, and mail fraud as soon as they took possession of that package.

The government had been trying for three years to pin Doris and John down to an address. They'd been trying for even longer to tie them to the profits generated by one of the most imaginative real-estate scams I've ever heard of. Doris and John, using publicly available land records, were able to provide banks with enough information on certain properties to secure loans against them. These loans were for a lot of money.

They ran this scam up and down the West Coast. Over the years, the only concrete trail Doris and John had left was the bank accounts they set up to help establish their bonafides — accounts they maintained for such a short period of time (a few months) that by the time they could be found and monitored, they'd stopped using them.

The authorities were able to access the records of one such account. They discovered that the Pooles had been sending large sums of money to a certain Leo Lukeman in New York City. Close to a dozen different checks, for a grand total in the high six figures.

The question was, why?

A federal agent friend of mine contacted me and asked that I do a little digging into Leo Lukeman's background. Who was he? Why was he getting money from the Pooles?

I discovered Leo was a legitimate businessman and the sole proprietor of a foreign currency exchange operation. And as a way to bring in a little extra money, he ran a commemorative coin business on the side.

THE POSTAL WATCH

Next time you're in the post office . . .

Walk up to one of the clerks and ask them if they know what a Postal Watch is. Odds are you'll receive the same answer I did at the Fort Lee, New Jersey, post office from not one, but half a dozen workers:

"A postal what?"

I got a similarly confused reaction from clerks in Ossining, New York, and Reston, Virginia. One postal clerk in Sante Fe, New Mexico, thought I was looking to buy a commemorative watch of some kind.

An older gentleman behind the counter in the Fort Lauderdale post office knew exactly what I was talking about, though.

"I can tell you about a Postal Watch," he said. "Helped out on one once."

I nodded for him to continue.

"It was maybe ten years ago — the Postmaster came in one morning and told me 'when the mail for Box 350 is all in, bring it to me in my office.' So I did. That afternoon, he stopped by again. 'What we did for Box 350 today — we'll do until further notice, got it? And this is just between the two of us.'

"So for about a week and a half I brought him the mail from Box 350 each morning. He took care of putting it back out when he was through. The mail was never really delayed. Some time later, I asked him what had been going on. The Postmaster said he'd gotten a call from a Postal Inspector up in Nashville and they suspected the guy renting 350 was up to something. So they wanted him on a Postal Watch."

At that point in time, the older gentleman explained, he had no idea what a Postal Watch was. So he asked. The Postmaster showed him how he'd had to keep a log of every piece of mail that came in to Box 350 that week, noting the sender, exactly who it was addressed to, the date it was received, postmark information, all markings or logos, and the type of mail (envelope, package, etc.) it was.

Let me add a few more details to that picture.

A Postal Watch can also be set up on a private home or a business.

A Postal Watch can also log your outgoing mail.

Any Postal Inspector, among other government employees and courts, can initiate one.

Odds are, too, that the local postal employees will be only too happy to help a Postal Inspector. And Postal Inspectors won't hesitate seeking the assistance of your neighborhood mailman. After all, who knows more about you than your mailman?

Imagine the following phone call:

"Yeah, this is Kevin McKeown — I'm a Postal Inspector up in Boston. Listen, I want you to put the household at 344 Dunham Street on a Watch. You'll get the paperwork tomorrow. Oh, and can you put their mailman on? Thanks. . . . Yeah, hi. Can you tell me about the family at 344 Dunham? How many kids they got? . . . OK. What about the house? Is it nice? Do they take care of it? . . . Good. What about cars? Many visitors? You think you can get the license plate numbers of any cars you see there this afternoon?"

Any soldier (postal employee) in the country's silent army can be mobilized at any time with a quick telephone call. Indeed, every postal delivery person is an on-site, knowledge-able investigator waiting to provide information.

A word about commemorative coins: You've probably seen them advertised in *Parade*, or *TV Guide*, or over the Internet. Somebody seems to mint one for almost every major occasion. The U.S. Mint issued the official Desert Storm coins. There are privately issued coins commemorating the kings of Hawaii and the King of Rock and Roll, and even coins that celebrate the fiftieth anniversary of aliens landing in Roswell, New Mexico.

Doris and John Poole, it turned out, had bought hundreds

of thousands of dollars' worth of these coins from Leo Lukeman. Why?

Well, the Pooles were very smart — and very careful with their illegally acquired fortune. They lived out of hotels and sublets and used a series of mail drops (such as Mailboxes, Etc.) and post office boxes for their return addresses. They lived modestly — they didn't make conspicuous, expensive purchases that would have drawn attention to them. And they made sure the money that they did use was thoroughly laundered.

Just to explain the term, "money laundering" means exactly that: taking dirty money and cleaning it so there is no trace of the source of the money. For example, drug dealers amass large piles of cash from the sale of drugs. A dealer might launder his ill-gotten money by depositing the cash in the bank account of a convenience store he has access to, controls, or owns. Usually, only a thorough audit by a good forensic accountant can backtrack and overcome the legalities and red tape surrounding the true origin of laundered money.

The Pooles laundered their huge illegal profits through commemorative gold coins.

Gold is portable money.

Gold is clean money. Just like diamonds and jewels, gold is easy to work with anywhere on earth. It's considered just as good as cash in conducting a financial transaction. And there is often the false perception that gold, silver, and jewels are legitimate, while a large pile of cash looks suspicious.

When the authorities discovered what the Pooles were up to, they decided to use Leo to get to them.

Which is how I came to be standing in his midtown office one afternoon, listening to a team of law enforcement officials explain that the next time he got an order from the Pooles, he should let them know.

Leo smiled. "This must be your lucky day."

He then disappeared into the back room. Half a minute later he came out, holding a stack of order forms, flipping through them as he walked.

"Ah-ha!" he said, handing one over to me. "Here it is."

He showed us the order form — along with the twenty-thousand-dollar check the Pooles had sent along. She had, like every previous order, given an actual street as the delivery address. Leo required that someone sign for the package upon delivery. This was, of course, a twenty-thousand-dollar package of gold. Doris thought she was prepared, but the mystery and crime novels she had been using as how-to guides were missing some crucial details.

This is where the Postal Inspectors entered the case.

Once Leo prepared the package, they were able to track it virtually every step of the way to its destination — down to the point of personally selecting the delivery man who would have the honor of bringing Doris and John their coins.

It looked like just another delivery in the quiet Hollywood hills. An innocent-looking mail truck stopping for a delivery. An even more innocent-looking postal delivery man, in a crisp blue shirt and official postal shorts, headed up the front walk carrying a clipboard and package.

The arrest went down virtually as planned — with one slight hitch.

The second Doris finished signing for the package, the Postal Inspectors and other federal agents began pouring up the hill to arrest her. They had to wait for the signature to ensure an innocent person, such as a maid, would not be used as a buffer between the authorities and the Pooles.

They made so much noise that John (who was just climbing out of a downstairs shower) managed to escape into the thick forest behind the house . . .

Wearing only his underwear.

That's a sight I would have loved to see.

❑ ❑ ❑ ❑ ❑

An ex-con once put it to me like this: "In the old days, you knew you were f***ed if the FBI or *60 Minutes* showed up.

Now, it's the Postal Inspectors."

Over the next few years, I suspect you'll be hearing a lot more about them. Previously charged with enforcing laws against wiretapping and mail fraud, their jurisdiction was recently extended into all forms of communication, including E-mail and the Internet. Which means that any act of fraud committed using those technologies is now classified as a federal crime.

Postal Inspectors have also played a major role in thwarting one of the nation's fastest-growing crimes: identity theft. We'll discuss this in greater detail in Chapter 11.

❑ ❑ ❑ ❑ ❑

Members of the post office perform one of the most vital tasks necessary to our existence and economic growth each and every day. They ensure the flow of information needed in commerce. They are indeed our friends. The problem is that mail, by its very existence, creates a big trail leading straight to each and every one of us.

❑ ❑ ❑ ❑ ❑

I was recently hired by a small manufacturing company in Manhattan that was being accused of committing securities fraud. The company (which must remain nameless) was receiving a lot of threatening mail from a particular law firm, representing a group of minority stockholders.

My job was to find out how seriously this complaint was being pursued, what resources (financial and personnel) the law firm and its clients were allocating to the case. Were they just barking loudly, or were they trying to bite?

The lawyer leading the complaint against my clients had, of course, identified himself in his correspondence. It took me about ten minutes of standing outside his law firm's mailroom to discover that the complaint was being very well financed. I saw letters going from the lawyer to ex-employees of the manufacturing company, various state and federal agencies, and several private investigators.

Once we learned how hard they were fighting, we began some correspondence of our own . . . but that's another story.

How many businesses do you know that plop outgoing mail in the lobby of their building in nice little bundles? Or leave their after-hours packages on the security guard's desk?

Take a walk through an office building on any given Saturday, and you'll find mail piled up neatly on the carpet outside most of their doors. A veritable mountain of information for those so inclined to rummage through.

Your personal outgoing mail can also reveal valuable information about you. Be careful how you send it.

Next time you're waiting in line at the post office, don't hold out your packages — with your carefully printed return address on them — for the world to see (remember the Mustard Man).

And when you put the flag up on your mailbox to let the postman know there's mail in there to be picked up, aren't you letting passersby know, too? An old trick by those who want to see your incoming or outgoing mail is to walk up to the curbside or front-door mailbox and, under the pretext of leaving a note in your mailbox, quickly flip through your mail.

WHAT COULD BE DONE

There's an easy solution to at least some of the privacy problems that currently exist at your mailbox, where any Tom, Dick, or Harriet can see who's sending you what with just a glance.

I believe the post office should deliver one envelope a day — a "Postal Privacy Pack." Filled and sealed at the post office, this one reusable, post office-issued envelope holds all your daily mail.

And speaking of envelopes . . .

Surely delivery services such as the post office, FedEx, UPS, etc., could put their "attempted delivery" notices inside a plain-looking envelope, rather than displaying to the world that they tried to drop off your expensive new computer but you weren't home. Those delivery slips stuck to your door aren't just a welcome sign for thieves — they also provide the clever con man with an opportunity to intercept your package.

The envelopes we send and receive should also reveal less information. How about the idea of a Postal General Mailing Address that can follow you wherever you move, an address tied in to the post office's increasingly sophisticated name and address database?

The Postal General Mailing Address (PGMA) would be an extension of the effective zip-plus-four system. When postal sorters scanned this letter/number code, up-to-date delivery routing information would be printed. Your address would read:

A1B2C3D4E5F6G7 - 12345 - 123456 - 123456789

The first series of letters/numbers would be your personal number; it would follow you everywhere.

The second and third series of numbers would be a codified number identifying the street number, street name and apartment/suite/room, etc., to be used by carriers for actual delivery.

The fourth series of numbers would be the current zip-plus-four number.

With this system you could alert the post office to the holding of mail, the temporary or permanent forwarding of mail, the refusal of certain type mail, etc., before it got to your home. This PGMA could be affixed to return labels, permanent ink stamps, or computer address databases. Of course, you'd still be able to have mail delivered the old-fashioned way. But any combination of the current addressing of mail and a numbering system could only assist in heightening privacy and timely mail delivery.

PLAY DETECTIVE

Develop a mail profile on a friend, relative, or coworker. Get their permission to review envelopes, magazines, and all other delivered mail, on the outside only. You can't open any mail or look inside.

Now, based on the information you've observed, profile this addressee. It should go something like this: "This person gets way too much mail. There are a lot of credit card bills; must be behind on a few with these 'personal and confidential' stamped envelopes. They belong to AAA. Ah, they must have a relative in Seattle. Oh, look at this. I see they must like _____ because of the mail they're getting from _____. Wh-o-o-oa, check this out. Ver-r-r-ry interesting! I never knew they _____. (Ouch! You get the point. Be nice. After you profile them, they get to profile you.)

PROTECT YOURSELF

1. **Have your mail delivered securely.** Once it leaves your postman's hands, make sure it can't be observed or, worse, stolen. A door mail slot or a locked curbside mailbox is essential. If you have a mail slot, make sure a person couldn't peek through and read the envelopes lying inside on the floor. Can a person simply standing outside your door see mail lying on a hallway table or kitchen counter?

2. **Send your important personal mail from a secure location.** If you have any concerns regarding your mail, don't leave outgoing mail in your mailbox for collection by the carrier. If there have been mail delivery thefts in your area or you have important financial or legal paperwork to mail, be careful. Hand items directly to your carrier or go to a local post office or post office mailbox.

3. **Have your most confidential mail delivered to an off-site location.** Consider using a post office box (by far the best choice), Mailboxes, Etc., or an alternate (friend's or coworker's) secure address.

4. Be careful when you're at the post office. Watch what you display to others waiting in line with you. Remember the Mustard Man. Read a newspaper and tuck that important, personal information under your arm: Don't display financial institutions you deal with, potential travel plans, legal matters, or addresses of distant relatives. Just the standard postal forms held in your hands will advertise the importance of what you're doing: Express Mail, insurance, certified mail, return receipt, etc. And watch what you throw out in the post office trash bin: personal notes on paper, receipts, addressed envelopes, postal money order receipts, etc. Especially vulnerable are those who frantically finish last-minute details while they are in line. They're too busy rushing and oblivious to potential con artists, etc.

5. Consider the full implications of filing a change-of-address form. If you file a change-of-address form you'll be jumping on the fattest and most sought-after mailing list train ever conceived. Databases everywhere will process, at lightning speed, the fact that you're a new, potential customer even before you move in. Decide who needs to know where you are moving and advise them accordingly. Or take the opportunity to redirect all of your mail to a more private address (a P.O. Box, etc.).

6. Don't stop your mail. Clever crooks watch for where the mailman doesn't deliver. Unless you have a secure, private mail slot that can handle two to three weeks' worth of regular mail, have a neighbor or friend pick up your mail.

7. Make a mental list of what is delivered to and sent out of your home by the post office and other delivery services. Profile yourself based on the mail you receive. What does that mail say about you and those who live with you?

8. Pressure businesses you deal with to use more discreet return mailing addresses, logos, etc. If you have a special concern or simply believe outsiders don't need to know your business, let those you deal with know how you feel. Consider drawing a big arrow pointing to a circled return address. Then write "Return to Sender. Privacy Violation." Plain brown envelopes aren't just for porno anymore.

9. Develop weekend and holiday mail procedures. This is especially true for businesses. Again, a secure environment (locked mail box, etc.) where the mail can be safely placed, and only accessed by those authorized, is the best defense against off-hour, holiday, and weekend roaming mail reviewers.

10. Conduct a mail security analysis. At home and at work. At work observe how the mail is delivered and follow the path of a day's mail. Where does it go? How does it get there? What evidence from the mail is left behind and where (trash)? At home, check your mail's delivery, vulnerability (it sits all day in the mailbox), review (piled up on the kitchen counter near the back window), and disposal (trash). Think of how easily you could steal or "borrow" a neighbor or competitor's mail. That's how easily it could be done to you.

11. Protect the information concerning the movement of your packages. Just like phone bills, I can tell a lot about what you're doing if I get my hands on your overnight package activity reports. Airborne, DHL, FedEx, UPS, and the post office can't guarantee you that no unauthorized person will come to possess your activity statements. For very sensitive material, pay cash, use a separate account with different mailing/billing/telephone information, or charge to a friend's account number and then reimburse them. If I want a million-dollar stock tip, I'll spend a few thousand on a company's overnight package activity report and see whom the

movers and shakers are communicating with. Use different messenger services, too. I was an undercover messenger once, and I learned some amazing information (and I appreciated the big tippers).

YOUR CREDIT CARDS

DINING AT ITS FINEST

These days, I travel too much to make joining a health club practical or worthwhile. I get my exercise by squeezing in an early morning run a few times a week. But several years back, when I was spending virtually all of my time in the New York metropolitan area, I was lucky enough to have a membership at one of the city's oldest, most exclusive athletic facilities.

At one point, I was going to the club five or six times a week, to relax as much as to work out. I could get a massage, use the steam room, lie by the pool, order dinner, or just sit around and watch TV. Eventually, I knew all the attendants by name.

Now this club wasn't like Bally's or Lucille Roberts: Joining got you the VIP treatment the second you walked in the door. One of the club's white-suited attendants would greet you by name — "Good afternoon, Mr. McKeown" (they would always call you "mister"), take your coat, and walk you over to your cubicle. This club's definition of "cubicle" was an enclosed area big enough for a bench, mirror, hangers for your clothes, shelves for your toiletries, and electrical outlets for your shaver, personal stereo, etc. The attendant would then personally escort you into the club proper.

Oh, I almost forgot.

Before you changed into your athletic gear, you would drop your valuables off with a "security guard." This guard was nothing more than another white-jacketed attendant who stood in a small fenced-in cage near the club's entrance. He would hand you a five-by-nine manila envelope. You would place your valuables inside, seal it, and write your name across the seal. The attendant then handed you a receipt in exchange for your envelope, which he made a big show of stapling shut with this huge, cranky old machine. The club's intention was to make you feel as if your valuables were as safe as they would be in Fort Knox.

Right.

One winter evening, I stopped in for a workout, beginning my visit by checking in at the security guard's desk.

"Good evening, Mr. McKeown," the attendant behind the cage said, handing me the requisite manila envelope.

I opened it and put in my valuables: my watch, the dollar bills and change I had in my pocket, and my wallet. I handed it back to the attendant, who then stapled the envelope shut. I took the receipt he gave me and went off to do my workout.

I started in the weight room. Then I ran on the indoor track. I hit the steam room, then ironed out some of the kinks in my neck in the spout room (a long, narrow room with a hose having the equivalent power of a firehose), and had a massage.

Finally, after a quick dip in the pool, I took the world's most relaxing nap in a poolside lounge chair. Listen to this, and see if your eyelids don't droop:

I started out by covering the lounge chair with a soft cotton sheet. One of the club's attendants then placed a towel over me. And on top of that came another cotton sheet, then a blanket, and, of course, a mask for my eyes. The hour's sleep I had in that chair left me feeling refreshed enough to start the day all over again.

Instead, I ordered dinner. Shrimp cocktail. Steak. And cheese-cake with coffee.

All served on fine china and wheeled in on a cart so that I could watch television in the small alcove next to the pool.

It was a luxurious evening. I ended it by getting dressed, going back to the cage, exchanging my receipt for my valuables, and making my way out onto the cold city streets — completely relaxed, physically and mentally . . .

Which was a good thing, because the next day I was suddenly on an assignment that sent me to Europe for three weeks. When I returned, I discovered a big envelope from Diner's Club in my mailbox. I thought they were sending out promotional paperbacks or one of those thick discount coupon books.

In fact, the envelope contained my bill for the previous month. My seven-thousand-dollar bill. It included charges at exclusive restaurants, stores, and theaters that I'd never been to in my life.

It was only then that I checked my wallet and discovered that my Diner's Club card was missing.

By checking my master list (see following sidebar), I determined that the only time my wallet was out of my possession during the entire month was during the one trip to the club.

The thieves must have opened the envelope, slid my wallet out, removed the one Diner's Club card, reinserted the wallet, and re-stapled the envelope. Smart. I would have noticed a lot earlier if they had taken the entire wallet.

A follow-up investigation by the fraud division of the credit card company revealed an identical complaint from another member of the same health club. The fraudulent charges in that case were similar to the ones billed to my card. Eventually the guilty parties were identified and prosecuted.

❑ ❑ ❑ ❑ ❑

Thanks to the Fair Credit Billing Act, cardholder liability in most instances of credit card fraud is limited to fifty dollars — as long as you notify the credit card company promptly of the theft.

Make discovering the theft easier on yourself. Don't carry around more cards than you need and keep track of how many cards you are carrying at all times.

THE MASTER LIST

Electronic fraud strikes in an instant and can be over in a blink of an eye. I can't tell you how to keep your credit card numbers completely safe. No one can. But what you can do is make sure that if a theft occurs, you notice it right away. The sooner you report the incident, the better chance authorities have of catching the thief.

The easiest way to distinguish fraudulent use of your card from legitimate charges is to keep a credit card master list. You can use a series of index cards; you can use a stenographer's notebook; you can use your computer — whatever works best for you. Remember that you'll want to write down your charges immediately after you incur them, so pick whatever is the most convenient.

Your credit card master list will contain three categories of information:

1) A list of all your credit cards — issuing bank, account number, 800-contact information, expiration date, and credit limit (it's a good idea to expand this to include a notation of all the information in your purse/wallet — keep a photocopy of your driver's license, Triple A account, etc.).

2) A record of each credit card transaction: date, card, amount, and location.

3) A record of every person and/or establishment you give

your credit card or your credit card number to (to reserve a hotel room, for example), and when you gave it.

When your credit card statement comes at the end of the month, check it against this list. You'll find out very quickly if an extra gas-tank fill-up or a second lunch has been added.

For those of you with expense accounts, here's a short cut you can use to check that all your restaurant charges are legitimate. When you leave a tip, use an amount that will make the grand total have the same last digit – say, 3. When you scan down your restaurant charges at the end of the month, make sure they all end in that number.

One reason a master list helps is that every charge statement you receive has a different billing format. Your eyes will be more likely to spot discrepancies against your familiar, personalized list — set up the way you like best.

Of course, it's not just the physical card you need to keep track of. The numbers associated with that card can also be compromised. . . .

WHAT'S MY LINE?

Maria Qualto was a waitress at Sparks (a New York City Upper East Side steak house, most famous for being the spot where mob boss Paul Castellano was gunned down). She had short dark hair and a French accent. None of the other wait staff got to know her very well in the month and a half she worked at the restaurant. She kept to herself, the manager told me.

Her social security number was 038-XX-6194.

Maria Qualto also worked at Rumpelmayer's, a Manhattan lunch institution, located on Central Park South near the Plaza

Hotel. She was a tall, thin, blond woman, who everyone thought looked exactly like Uma Thurman. "The customers loved her," the manager there said. "I can't understand how she could get involved in something like this."

Her social security number — or rather, the social security number she gave when she filled out her employment card — was also 038-XX-6194.

And Maria Qualto worked at Odeon, a downtown bistro that is the late-night place to see and be seen. She was a young girl — not much older than twenty — who seemed to genuinely love her job and the excitement that went with it. Her coworkers were surprised when she walked in one afternoon and, without offering any explanation, simply quit.

Her SSN? You guessed it: 038-XX-6194.

All these Maria Qualtos — as well as four others I discovered in the course of the investigation — were part of a scam pulled by the most organized, creative group of credit card thieves I've ever come across.

I came into this case at the request of a very well-connected Manhattan lawyer — a one-time politician who had left public life for greener pastures. Several of his clients, including an aid to the police commissioner, three police inspectors and a deputy mayor, had discovered extra charges on their credit card accounts. The charges were for meals at restaurants they often frequented, but hadn't eaten at on the days in question.

My first thought was that the restaurants themselves were running some kind of credit card scam. A manager, or an assistant manager, was taking cash from one customer, pocketing it, and then using a regular customer's card number to pay the bill so the restaurant's accounts balanced out. Those regulars wouldn't (hoped the scamster) notice the extra charges on their bills.

There were a lot of clients involved — and a lot of charges. I hired some help, and we started interviewing the managers at the restaurants that had been hit.

At the first restaurant we visited, we discovered that half a dozen members of the wait staff had left the week after the fraudulent charges. Anyone in the restaurant business knows that there's a lot of turnover, but this smelled funny. Especially when added to the fact that every waiter whose name could be connected to a fraudulent credit card slip was gone.

Among those who moved on was a waitress named Maria Qualto.

There was also a Maria Qualto at the next restaurant we visited. Or rather, there had been a Maria Qualto. She too (the thin blond one) had left suddenly.

As I said, we discovered seven Maria Qualtos altogether. And they not only had the same social security number, but they all lived within a few blocks of each other.

We started at Maria Qualto #1's residence — a large two-bedroom, duplex apartment in Queens, filled with the cheapest furniture imaginable. The neighbors told us a half-dozen youngish, fairly sophisticated, attractive people had lived in the apartment, all of whom had moved out a few weeks back.

We found virtually the same situation at Maria Qualto #2's house. After a few more days of painstaking investigation, the broad outlines of the scam emerged. The ring consisted of men and women in their twenties who were all illegal immigrants. Cultured illegal immigrants — polite, well spoken (with the slightest hint of an accent — which all the restaurant managers loved), and very attractive.

These immigrants used false identification, and several of them shared a single identity. Which is how Maria Qualto could work in seven different restaurants at the same time. Each Maria kept her salary and tips, kept copious notes on the regulars in restaurants, and made duplicate imprints of the customer's credit cards.

The actual hit — the short period of time when the bogus charges were put through — was orchestrated with the agility of an O'Hare air traffic controller in a thunderstorm. Each waiter pocketed as much cash as possible and replaced it with a corresponding credit card charge. Daily restaurant accounting always checked out. Only one restaurant owner voiced some suspicion, stating that although business appeared constant, "more people are using those damn credit cards."

The ringleaders knew that they had a limited window of opportunity, namely one complete billing cycle for each card. If, for whatever reason, the credit card companies themselves reviewed any of the cardholders' charge patterns (which fraud departments regularly do), it would be consistent with their normal spending habits.

After the hit, the waiters and waitresses quit their jobs, were given a "bonus" and bused out of town with new fake ID papers.

The total take? I can't be sure — but it was at least a quarter-million dollars.

The scam was arranged down to the tiniest detail. The police never realized the scope of the crime until much later, because 1) the victims were reluctant to publicize the fraud at all because doing so would reveal how much time and taxpayer money had been spent at these high-class restaurants, and 2) neither the customers nor the restaurants lost money — only the credit card companies.

The next time you wonder why those companies have to charge up to 18 percent interest, remember this story.

❑ ❑ ❑ ❑ ❑

Big-ticket fraud is usually easy to spot. It's the small "unauthorized" charges consistent with your usual buying patterns that are the problem. And even if you manage to catch those, there are other ways your credit card information can be used against you:

You can be victimized by a second cardholder on your account. For example, say your daughter has a school acquaintance over who happens to see a credit card statement lying around.

With a little perseverance, she can request that a second card — in her name, on your account — be sent to her. You'll never find out about it . . . until she doesn't pay.

Then it's your credit that's ruined.

Other visitors to your home, a painter or the plumber's

assistant, may find the monthly statements you left lying out on the kitchen counter.

With the explosion of at-home catalog shopping and the growth of on-line businesses, millions of people give out their credit card information on a daily basis, on the telephone and on the Internet — when you order Braves tickets or that new shirt from the L. L. Bean catalog.

Numbers can be stolen months before they're ever used. For example, you place an order with a mail-order computer company, giving them your credit card information over the phone. The person who takes your order (or their unsavory coworker) simply makes note of those numbers. It's like money in the bank after a few weeks or months. It's very, very difficult for investigators to make the connection between the original theft and the use of the card information when months lapse in between.

Also, the dramatic rise in credit card transactions (up 96 percent over the last two years) means that those numbers are sitting in more and more databases around the country.

Remember the paparazzi analogy from Chapter 5 — the people who are stalking the celebrities hoping to find a juicy tidbit to sell to the media? It holds true here, too. There's a whole industry of people out there, combing through the records of what you buy and whom you buy it from, assembling an increasingly comprehensive profile of you. Mail-order catalog companies swap addresses with firms who sell to a similar demographic; pharmacies sell the names and addresses of pregnant women to diaper manufacturers.

Everyone's getting in on this act. Evangelist Oral Roberts purchased a list of people who had recent credit trouble from a database firm and promptly offered to intercede with God on their behalf if they'd send a donation to his foundation.

BIG BROTHER IS WATCHING

The largest provider of information has been, and continues to be, the government.

Remember that last piece of personal data on your driver's license that we talked about in Chapter 4 – your picture?

By the time you read this, your state may have sold it to a company called Image Data, LLC of Nashua, New Hampshire. Image is building a national database of such photos, using a loophole in the recently passed federal Driver's Privacy Protection Act to purchase photos directly from state motor vehicle departments without citizen approval.

They intend to use this "TrueID" technology to stop credit card and check fraud by transmitting your photo straight to a computer screen at the cash register.

Image owes you $1.5 million worth of thanks for helping finance this program. You, the taxpayer, paid for this by way of the Secret Service — who hopes the technology can be used to fight terrorism and immigration abuse, and who supplied the cash from its budget.

Citizens interested in preventing this use of driver's license photos should E-mail their congressman. Image will pay the state one penny for your image, but the cost to you in aggravation and loss of privacy will be much higher than that. If nothing else, you should be given a choice.

WHAT COULD BE DONE

Image isn't the only company taking the high-tech road to credit card fraud protection. Citibank (light years ahead of the pack at the moment) issues customers bankcards (credit and debit) with their photo imprinted on the back.

Given how quickly anti-fraud technology is evolving, within a few years it's doubtful that much credit card fraud will exist at all. Through photo ID, fingerprint analysis (the most secure and cost-effective method), voice recognition, retina scan, PIN numbers, or a combination of these methods, your identification will be verified beyond a shadow of a doubt at the point of purchase.

Another immediately achievable method of high-tech fraud prevention would involve the use of full hologram credit cards. Instead of the decorative symbols that now adorn your card, your actual credit card information (name and number) would be embedded within a hologram. This hologram would only be visible when viewed at the proper angle and at close proximity.

And though they are not exactly credit cards, the new check cards — cards that act like a plastic check, with the charge debited directly from your checking account — are also helping consumers. For one thing, you're more likely to notice fraudulent activity because you tend to keep closer track of your checking account. There isn't even the potential fifty-dollar maximum charge for fraudulent charges on a check card because the transaction is processed like a check instead of a credit card.

One protection that credit card companies could immediately institute, allowing you to become more involved in the prevention of fraud, is a personal control option available through the current 800 number customer service lines that allow you to access your account. Say, for example, your credit limit is three thousand dollars. The personal control option would allow you to limit charges to your card in any twenty-four-hour period to, for example, two hundred dollars or even fifty dollars. Now, if you know you will be using your credit card to charge more than the temporary limit you've designated, you would simply telephone the card company's 800 number, enter your account number, a PIN code, and possibly the anticipated amount to be charged. You would, in essence, be pre-approving your own anticipated charges. It's not foolproof, but it's an option that could be immediately programmed into credit card computer systems and have a significant impact on the total dollar amount of any given fraud. It could put another desperately needed hurdle in front of a thief.

Telephone calling cards, which are the most abused of any charge card, should immediately be required to have this option. You would program a daily limit into a computer system and, again, simply increase this limit at any time by the same method above. Another choice in the personal control option would prohibit international telephone calls until cleared by your authorizing procedure with a PIN code. This would just about shut down international telephone fraud as we know it today. In effect, your telephone calling card would become as safe as the ever increasingly popular prepaid calling cards.

These kinds of antifraud measures should enable credit card companies to lower their costs — and their interest rates — considerably (as I said earlier, there's a reason they have to charge 18 percent, or more, interest). But don't hold your breath.

PLAY DETECTIVE

Your assignment: Obtain three telephone calling card numbers and two credit card numbers by just watching and listening to people either at a pay phone or at a retail store. Be nosy, be observant, and get that information. Don't write it down, just read or listen to the information. See for yourself how easy it is. Then, in a friendly, helpful way, say to the person whose card information you obtained, "I couldn't help but hear/see your credit card information. There's a lot of credit card fraud out there. You should be more careful. I hear a lot of people are getting ripped off. I know I'm concerned."

PROTECT YOURSELF

1. Keep a master list. Carry it with you or keep it in a convenient place where you'll use it. Make a quick and simple note of each charge — date, amount, and place — and each time you supply your card number (to hold airline tickets, for instance).

2. Minimize the number of credit cards you have. The fewer statements you have to pay attention to, the better chance you'll have of spotting any irregular activity. Try getting rid of just one card within the next thirty days. Then try it again.

3. Safeguard your credit card information. Treat your credit card statements like you would a wad of cash. Keep them in a safe place, not out in the open for visitors, repairmen, etc., to observe. Never simply discard a charge card statement in the trash basket. (Refer back to the trash stories in Chapter 2.)

4. Consider not carrying a wallet. Instead of that mini-filing cabinet you lug around, take only the essentials: driver's license, ID, and the one or two credit cards you might have need for. Carry these cards and ID with your cash in your front pocket. You'll protect them better. If you really have to carry a wallet, never keep it in one of your back pockets.

5. Make a copy of the cards you carry with you. Copy the complete contents of your wallet/pocketbook as well. Seal the copies in an envelope and file them. These will come in handy if your cards are lost or stolen.

6. Check with credit card companies and make sure there are no unauthorized secondary cardholders on your accounts. Tell your credit card company you want periodic (three or four times a year), written advisement of the existence and status of secondary cards for which you might be held responsible.

7. Test your frequent charges. Make sure all of your regular charges — restaurant, gasoline, certain services, etc. — end with a specified digit, if possible. This will reveal unauthorized charges at a glance. Test the vendors you use most. They just might have a dishonest employee. Save your receipts (number them each time you get one if possible). This is most important for accounts with many charges. It's hard to detect a bogus seventeen-dollar gas charge to your account if it's hidden among many legitimate items.

8. Require your credit card companies to advise you in writing when an inquiry about your credit card is made or a change is requested. This includes second cards, credit limit increases, and address changes. An old trick scamsters use is to call the credit card company and change your mailing address two months before your current card expires. Guess where the company mails the new card? It is currently very easy to discuss and change crucial account information by telephone.

9. Insist that all charge card companies require a secret code or PIN before they discuss any information over the telephone. This includes telephone calling cards. Request that a written advisement be sent to you every time information is given out by one of their representatives.

10. Help the dead. "Borrowing" a deceased person's credit information is a widespread problem. Make sure all credit bureaus and credit card companies the deceased was affiliated with are advised of the death in writing.

YOUR COMPUTER

LET'S GET TOGETHER AND FEEL ALL RIGHT: THE EASE OF ELECTRONIC THEFT

"My name is Anthony Barstow," I said, sitting down. I made a show of brushing a nonexistent piece of lint off my precisely creased trousers. "I'm his assistant."

"Well," the young woman across from me — she'd introduced herself as Juanita Ramos a moment ago, and the nameplate on her desk identified her as the bank's Information Services Specialist — said as she turned to her computer and keyed in a few commands. "Let's check the records. It'll just take a few seconds."

"Thank you so much," I said, glancing at my watch, creating, I hoped, the very picture of the impatient businessman, to whom every second mattered.

In fact, I was in no real hurry. The sun was streaming in through the window behind me, warming my back. Outside, tourists and natives alike were walking past, laughing and enjoying themselves on this relaxing summer afternoon.

Just another happy day in Jamaica — home of reggae music, Blue Mountain coffee, numerous vacation resorts . . . and the money our friend, the really bad bald man from Chapter 5, was trying to hide from his ex-wife.

You may recall those calls to Jamaica listed on the phone records we'd subpoenaed, which we traced to a fax machine. A fax machine somewhere in the very bank I was now sitting in.

I'd taken the ninety-minute flight from Miami into Montego airport earlier that morning. When I arrived at the bank, I introduced myself and was taken to Ms. Ramos. I told her that my employer — the bad bald man, I mean, Benny — was expecting a large sum of money to be wired into his account and was very anxious to know if it had arrived.

In order to wire money into an individual's account, you need two key numbers: the bank's routing information and the individual's account number. The routing number is not confidential information; the account number is.

The account number was what I was after. With it, I could access Benny's bank records by telephone and prove to the judge that he had out-and-out lied about his assets.

Because I knew his name, his date of birth, his mother's maiden name, etc., I was able to convince Ms. Ramos that I was Benny's assistant. She began to pull up his records on her screen without a second thought.

"Here it is now," Ms. Ramos said, looking at her monitor. "No. I don't see any recent transfers."

"Really?" I asked. "That's odd."

"Nothing there," she said.

"He's going to be very upset," I said.

Ms. Ramos shrugged. "I don't know what to say to you. Maybe it's on its way."

What I was hoping she would say to me was something like "see for yourself," and turn the computer monitor to face me, so I could read it off the screen.

That didn't seem likely. Even though she'd accepted me as Benny's assistant, Ms. Ramos wasn't letting me have any information that could be construed as confidential. And if I gave her even the slightest indication that I didn't know my employer's account number, her suspicions would instantly be aroused. She might even report my attempt to get the information to the bad bald man — which would let him know that someone was on to his little hideaway, and send him scurrying off to find a new place to hide his money.

I studied her closely for a moment. Juanita Ramos couldn't have been more than twenty-five years old, a skinny, dark-skinned woman in a bright, floral print dress, trying very hard to look and act like an important bank executive.

Heartless snooper that I am, I felt only a momentary twinge of guilt when I considered how I was about to take advantage of her.

"Well," I said, standing. "I'm going to have to call them tonight and make sure it gets in tomorrow. Because he's very concerned that everything be in place at the bank here."

"Of course," Ms. Ramos said.

"Will you be here tomorrow?"

"Yes, yes," she said. "I'm here all day."

"Good," I said. I held out my hand. "Thank you so much for your help, Ms. Ramos."

"You're welcome," she said, without moving from her desk.

"Oh." I stopped, as if I had just thought of something. "You know what? You have your bank's routing number there — let me make sure we didn't send the money to the wrong bank."

And before she could say a word, I leaned forward, swiveled her computer monitor around so that it faced me, and wrote down the bank's routing information — as well as the bad bald man's account number. Now I carefully zipped up my day-planner and swiveled the monitor around again to face her.

"I'll speak to you tomorrow, Ms. Ramos," I said. "A pleasure."

Three hours later I was back in Miami, faxing my clients Benny's account number.

❑ ❑ ❑ ❑ ❑

Ever seen a pickpocket at work? The good ones are like artists — they can be standing in the middle of a crowded subway train, simultaneously smiling at a pretty girl and pulling a wallet out of a businessman's back pocket.

Odds are, if you've had an experience with a pickpocket, it has been after the fact — that sickening moment when you reach for your wallet only to discover you've been robbed. What's worse, you have no idea when it happened. You didn't see, hear, or feel a thing. You had no idea you were in danger.

Your experience with electronic theft will be exactly the same.

All the personal, supposedly private data we've talked about in previous chapters — your public records, your phone records, your credit card accounts, as well as a great deal of other confidential information on you, such as your medical records, consumer profile, etc. — now exists as part of a database somewhere. Even as you read this, that information is being transmitted back and forth between various computers, analyzed and re-analyzed, bought, sold, and resold. At every step of the way, that personal information is subject to being compromised.

And not just by the high-tech hackers you read about in the paper.

No matter how many different passwords, levels of document encryption, or redundant security features are built into a computer system, that system's only as secure as the people watching over it choose it to be . . .

People like the businessman's secretary, who writes her boss's password on a notepad next to the monitor. The programmers, who build the same back door into every system they design. Even the good-intentioned Ms. Ramos.

So what can be done?

WHAT COULD BE DONE

Even before you were born, you were a number: one pending birth. And you definitely, eventually, would become another kind of number, a death statistic. It is impossible to separate ourselves from numbers. Numbers give structure, guidance, and purpose to our lives. We need numbers, the universal language, to survive.

But we avoid being identified with a number because it seems to reduce our individuality and uniqueness. However, we did choose to barter a small bit of our individuality for the promise of a social security retirement check. We are now identified nationally by a social security number.

Using the social security number as a multipurpose ID number happened by accident. The need to track people with some kind of numbering system grew at blinding speed. The only organized system that existed was the system used by the social security administration. So it was borrowed. But like many books that are borrowed, it was never returned. And it should have been.

To use a nine-digit number like the social security number to address today's need for a national identification number is, very politely stated, insane. It simply doesn't work. Your social security number is in no way confidential. It's in many, many databases. Any desire to associate privacy with a social security number is abandoned at the time a person registers to vote. When you fill in your social security number on the voter registration form, it becomes part of the public record, available for review by anyone. Also, the first few times a social security number is provided to any person or entity for commercial reasons ensures its availability to the public.

We need a system that will provide the government with the information it requires and address the needs of commerce while satisfying the privacy concerns of businesses and ordinary citizens. A useful personal identification number has been hinted at for years. Legislators have wasted many hours debating the issue. And still we don't have one — a national ID number. Technology and the alarming attack on our privacy makes a national ID number now more essential than ever.

AN IMMODEST PROPOSAL

Since the government loves acronyms so much, let's call it a NIDAC number — a National IDentification ACcount number. I'm proposing a multilevel NIDAC system that would put control of your most personal records — your medical data, your employment history, your driving record, your financial records — back in your hands. You would decide who would be granted access to almost every piece of information. (There is some information that you just can't withhold, like real estate-related information, for example. If nothing else, you would at least be notified that a request for information had been made.)

Every person and business would have a NIDAC number that would consist of, possibly, a combination of letters and numbers, or a simple twenty-digit number. I say "simple" because it would be set up like two telephone numbers. For example, 202-223-8030-202-223-5204. The cadence, rhythm and familiarity of recalling a telephone number should be utilized. Surely, we can all remember two new telephone numbers!

The first ten digits of the NIDAC could loosely be compared to the existing nine-digit social security number — not very private or protected. The real privacy protection follows with the second ten digits.

This system would have four different levels, with increasing degrees of protection for your personal information. Essential is the requirement that you be notified of a request for your information and that the requester be clearly identified. The dissemination of information about you needs to be put back in your control, or, at the very least, positioned to be monitored by you.

Level 4 provides notice and requestor identification. When Level 4 information is accessed, you would be given notice of the request and the identity of the requestor. Level 4 information would consist of your consumer profile — the kind of targeted information marketers and businesses so greatly desire. It would be your choice, for example, whether your telephone number is at this level and available to telemarketers. The exchange of Level 4 information would be possible with the first ten digits of an individual's or business's NIDAC number.

Level 3 provides notice, requestor identification, and an objection period during which you can challenge the dissemination of certain information. Level 3 information would include your civil records, real estate records, business affiliations, tax liens, business licenses, commercial loans, etc. — information that is now generally available and, most likely, should continue to be. The difference with this system is that you would be notified when someone requests information about you and you would have a specified period of time to challenge the request's fulfillment. Of course, you would be allowed to immediately waive the waiting period to facilitate any exchange of information.

Level 2 provides for your approval before information is released. You would advise the NIDAC system in writing or by a telephone PIN code that a certain person or entity is permitted either complete or partial Level 2 information. Or the system would contact you upon receipt of a request and await your approval. Level 2 information could include your biography, home address, home telephone, credit data, voting registration, school records, your picture, employment records, vehicle registration, and driver's license information.

Level 1 includes the most personal of information. Level 1 information would include your financial data (banking, investment, retirement, taxes, etc.) and marital, government file, adoption, medical, and criminal data. Requestors at Level 1 would be required to provide ID along with your verifiable approval. Again, the release of partial or complete Level 1 information would be your choice.

An important part of the NIDAC system includes NIDACs for business entities. Imagine the homeowner who could access a picture of a contractor, the firm's Better Business Bureau profile, and verification of a proper license.

Access to NIDAC information could be by mail, fax, or Internet for the transactions requiring a PIN. The more secure-level data could be made available only at kiosks located at police stations or other state offices, federal offices, or post offices.

Who is going to administer the NIDAC program? It has to be a division of the Justice Department. The profit motive needs to be taken out of any system that controls our most personal and private information. The only system that is relatively secure is NCIC — The National Crime Information Center. It's where national criminal data is collected, monitored, properly organized, and disseminated. The NCIC is light years ahead of the so-called privacy practices of the IRS.

A final thought. For those who look at the NIDAC system and see Big Brother's reach lengthening, I say get over it. All the information in this section is already out there, now being spread about recklessly. True reform will provide what is really needed: notice, accountability, and choice.

The misguided and archaic Big Brother fears have been fueled by those on both sides of the debate. The joke is that the government has been looking at way more than you really know for way longer than you think. And thank goodness it has. There's a good reason terrorists haven't struck more often in this country. You should be more appreciative of Big Brother and understand it's not *Big* Brother's watching that ought to concern you. It's the *bad* brother's actions all around us that should have us worried.

OFFICE POLITICS

"We think it's one of our competitors." The chief of security — an ex-cop named Bobby Wormelston — leaned forward in his chair and steepled his hands on the table. "I can give you a list of who the most likely suspects are."

I'd been brought in by Crane Brothers — an investment banking firm located in midtown Manhattan — to find out who'd sent a series of nasty, obscene, and threatening faxes to several members of the firm. Those faxes were full of inside information on a number of pending deals.

The company had kept the situation quiet, but they were more than a little concerned. Had their communications system been compromised? To find out, they had brought in a top-flight electronics expert experienced in corporate terrorism, who had swept their phone lines for bugs. They hadn't found anything (confirming my feelings about the effectiveness of such sweeps in general). If somebody knows what he's doing, you're not going to catch him with a sweep.

The fact that Wormelston had recommended the sweep brought him down a notch in my opinion. In fact, the more I worked on this case, the more I realized that he was in way over his head.

To me, the inside information in the faxes immediately suggested one thing.

"Have you thought about the possibility it's someone within the company?" I asked.

"I don't think so," Wormelston began. "It seems. . . ."

"We have considered the possibility," the man at the head of the table interrupted. He was John Crane, the company's chief operating officer. "And for now, it doesn't make sense to rule anybody out."

I agreed with Crane.

Crane Brothers was a fairly small firm — a couple dozen employees — and for the next several hours, I went over the company's personnel files with Crane and Wormelston. An investment banking firm does business in a pressure-cooker kind of environment — the competition for client dollars is intense and often takes place not just between firms, but within the company. A lot of money is at stake, and there are a lot of opportunities to make enemies, making the inside-man scenario even more probable.

I started interviewing Crane's employees right away. Almost immediately, my suspicions centered on a junior-level executive named Edward Simon for a variety of reasons, chief of which was an argument he'd had a few weeks back with another employee. Simon, normally a quiet man, had virtually exploded at his coworker, and though he'd calmed down quickly, he'd revealed a temper few had suspected he had.

The interviews revealed no definite evidence, however, so Crane arranged for me to have after-hours access to the company's offices, which took up an entire floor in a high-rise office building just off Sixth Avenue.

I arrived at Crane's offices shortly after midnight (just after the cleaning staff left) with a box of Dunkin' Donuts, a thermos of coffee, and an expert computer technician. We stayed until 6 A.M. — just before Crane's employees usually began arriving.

Starting in Simon's office, my expert looked at all the computers on the floor, scanning every sector of every hard drive for traces of the offending correspondence.

While he was combing through various bits and bytes, I was digging in wastebaskets — more precisely, going through the trash the cleaning staff had collected, again paying particular attention to Simon. I found suggestions of a heated interoffice romance, traces of employee dissatisfaction in the form of a discarded resume, and a lot of empty coffee cups. But no hints as to the source of the faxes.

Working nights for a week straight, my computer guy made the same lack of progress.

If Simon was the guilty party (and the more I worked on the case, the more I became convinced that despite the lack of evidence, he was our man), he was hiding his tracks carefully. He must have been erasing his computer keystrokes almost as he typed them.

But how were we going to catch him in the act? We couldn't very well sit in his office with him every second of the working day, looking over his shoulder.

Or could we?

The next night, we set up a video camera focused on Simon's desk. Although he mostly used the desktop computer, he always had his laptop with him. We needed to tape everything he typed on either screen. When we looked at that tape the following day, we had him.

When shown the videotape, Simon had no choice but to confess to sending the faxes. He did it, he said, to frighten other members of the firm away from the lucrative deals he wanted to make.

Needless to say, Simon never made those — or any other deals — for Crane Brothers.

❏ ❏ ❏ ❏ ❏

Computers have become an integral part of the American workplace. And you have the same privacy rights with regard to the data in your office computer as you do with regard to the phone records we discussed in Chapter 5.

Zero.

Be careful what kind of information you keep in there. It's no safer than a hard-copy printout would be.

In fact, if your computer is connected to a network (unlike Edward Simon's) or if someone has the necessary software that's now available, another monitor three floors above your office can be programmed to mirror every keystroke as it occurs.

Be aware of what's visible on your screen, both when you're in your office and when you're not. The last thing you want is someone walking in at lunch to drop off a memo and seeing your resume or that confidential letter you were working on. And remember, your coworkers aren't the only ones with access to your office.

Last year, I was investigating two Indian businessmen in London who were suspected of swindling dozens of U.S. investors. There was no paper trail — their trash consisted of what they had for lunch. Their office building was packed with security guards; there were cameras everywhere. It was as tight an operation as I'd ever encountered anywhere in the world.

My partner on this case and I began hanging out around their building on a regular basis — riding the elevator at different times of the day and roaming around on various floors so the security staff would get the idea we belonged there.

And so we could get a feel for when the cleaning staff came around.

After a few weeks, we were able to determine how many people were in the clean-up crew and who was responsible for our targets' office. Our quickly anointed partner, unbeknownst to her, would be an older woman who spoke maybe half-a-dozen words of English. The cleaning woman.

YOUR E-MAIL

In most companies, e-mail has virtually replaced the interoffice memo. It's fast, informal, and with the advent of laptop computing, puts you in the thick of things even if you're on vacation a thousand miles away.

But that convenience is a double-edged sword.

If you followed the government's antitrust case against Microsoft, you're aware of the central role e-mail played in that case — and how people's words are coming back to haunt them. Off-the-cuff remarks are now being presented in court as corporate policy. (Some companies have already begun taking steps to protect themselves against similar occurrences. Amazon.com, for one, has instituted a formal policy restricting the things that can be expressed in corporate e-mail.)

Here's a good way to keep yourself out of trouble when you're writing e-mail: Make believe a copy of everything you write is going directly to your boss or a reporter at your local newspaper, TV station, or radio station.

It's not just what you put in your e-mail message that needs protection. Your e-mail address can be a valuable commodity to businesses seeking to use the Internet as a marketing tool. Every site you visit is a potential seller (and reseller) of your e-mail address. There are software programs that roam the Internet, automatically gathering up e-mail addresses by the tens of thousands to be sold to budding entrepreneurs.

Remailing services and other technological tricks allow you to send out e-mail anonymously. Just know that you're usually leaving a trail.

❑ ❑ ❑ ❑ ❑

When my partner and I, dressed in suits and engaged in a vigorous argument about work, squeezed past the maintenance cart that had been holding the office suite door open, this poor woman immediately went into a subservient mode. Particularly when my partner started yelling about how "his" office had been filthy a few days ago. A nasty ploy, but it worked.

While she was occupied, I simply took a stack of diskettes out of my pocket and copied everything I could off the hard drive, including all e-mail communication. We got the next flight out.

Our case against the Indian gentlemen proceeded very nicely from that point on.

ERASE VS. DELETE:
DISCARD VS. DESTROY

Data stored on a computer comes with all sorts of technological vulnerabilities. Just ask Monica Lewinsky, who found the love notes to President Clinton she thought she'd erased being used as the centerpiece of Ken Starr's prosecution of the president.

If you want to erase files — and make sure the data is really gone — don't just delete them. There is a big difference between erase and delete in the computer world. "Delete" just means "not seen or easily retrievable." Just see how easily you can undelete something in any program or computer.

But wait, what happens when you really erase something?

Well, not much there, either. The biggest computer misperception (and possibly the fourth biggest lie) is the belief that "erase" means "gone — forever." It's like losing a watch. It's gone from your perspective but it's still out there, probably being used by someone else. There's always a chance, albeit slim, that you'll get it back.

Your choices are limited if you want computer data gone forever — destroyed.

You can use magnets to corrupt every speck of data on any kind of hard or tape drive or on storage accessories (diskettes, tapes, etc.). This is not recommended. It doesn't always completely do the job.

Or you can perform the only task that is known to be completely effective: Physically and completely destroy that hard drive, tape drive, diskette, tape, etc. Destroy, as in remove, beat with a hammer into little pieces, and then discard.

Sure, you can reformat your hard drive — in an attempt to write over every used and unused sector. But you'd be wasting your time. Or you can even go that extra step with the "format: c/v/u" command (this formats the c drive, then verifies the procedure (v) to ensure that a universal (u) rewrite was accomplished.) Not good enough. You can use some of the commercially available software programs that "wipe" or "purge" everything. Don't believe it. Recovering what you thought was gone may be difficult, but it can be done.

Again, there is only one sure way to make sure computer information is really destroyed and that is to really destroy it. Period.

Think of the motivation of the person or entity that wants the data in your computer, then think what that data means to you. Only then can you decide if you want to get rid of your computer or live with the possibility of the data being discovered.

THE GAMES PEOPLE PLAY

Last year, I helped a friend of mine out by taking her nine-year-old daughter to play in her regular Sunday afternoon soccer game. During the match, I stood next to a tall, balding man, who was chain-smoking and pacing back and forth on the sideline.

"That's my daughter," he said, halfway through the game, pointing to a girl on the field who seemed to have inherited his nervousness, judging by the way she kept overshooting her teammates when trying to pass. The man and I soon struck up a conversation, and somehow the talk turned to computers.

We talked about different brands, different programs, different games. We talked about how powerful computers were, how powerful they were going to get. We even talked about how they controlled, or were going to control, every aspect of your life.

I shouldn't really say "we" talked. This guy monopolized the conversation, barely letting me get a word in. I drifted off for a little bit, watching the kids play soccer while he went on about how Microsoft's stranglehold on the computer industry was a good thing, and something about computer stocks, and suddenly he was saying:

"I'm real security conscious."

"Really?" I asked, turning to him. Now he had my attention.

"Oh, yeah," he said. "Especially when it comes to computers." He took a deep puff on his cigarette. "Don't ever buy anything over the Internet — it's not safe."

"Mmmm," I nodded. "Is that so?"

He nodded right back. "They can get your credit card numbers and go to town." He took another drag. "It's just not safe being on-line."

I didn't want to interrupt him (why start now, I figured) by telling him that as far as I knew, having your credit card numbers stolen was just about the least of your worries when it came to on-line security.

Then he proceeded to tell me a story that demonstrated the

point better than anything I could have said.

"I was on-line the other day," he began, "when all of a sudden this little window pops up on my screen. And it says, 'Watch out! The contents of your hard drive are being scanned.'"

"Really?" I said. My eyebrow went up. I'd never heard of anything like that happening.

"Yeah," he said. "And then a list of everything on my computer — every file, every program — started scrolling down my screen in that little window."

"Wow," I said — and meant it.

"Wow," he agreed. "Then, when it was done scrolling, another little window popped up. And it said, 'This is how hackers can get into your computer. Protect yourself — order Safeguard for only $39.95.'" He shrugged, "Then the window disappeared."

"So," I said. "Did you order it?"

He shrugged, threw his cigarette down, and stomped it out.

"Nah," he said. "Too expensive."

We finished watching the game in silence.

❑ ❑ ❑ ❑ ❑

Odds are, if you have a personal computer at home, one of its primary uses is to explore the Internet.

I don't know if something like the above has ever happened to you, but I have the feeling that most people are just as cavalier about the danger being on-line presents to your personal computer data as Soccer Dad.

I'm not a computer expert, but I've worked with the best, in business and in the government. And I know that wherever you go on-line, you leave a record. Your Internet browser (Microsoft Internet Explorer or Netscape Navigator) sends an electronic message — the term is "cookie" — to every site you visit. That cookie announces to the owner of the site who you are.

You can disable cookies in your preferences or options file but it doesn't eliminate every trace of your travels. You can ask your computer to notify you each time a site you visit requests a cookie (do this for an illuminating look at what happens each time you visit a Web site). But don't think this protects you; it's just telling you what happened.

Intel's new Pentium III processor (at the time of this writing, THE state-of-the-art personal computer chip) contains a feature that recently had privacy advocates up in arms. Each chip was designed to transmit its serial number over the Internet and identify the computer user wherever he went on-line. Intel finally agreed to disable — but not remove — the feature. Those IDs have existed in computer software for some time, even if they've never received the publicity the Intel chip did. Microsoft Windows 98 and Office 97 contained unique identifiers, which were designed to prevent unauthorized duplication of the programs, but also enabled their users to be tracked. Every one of Apple's new iMAC computers contains a similar feature.

How can you keep this kind of identifying information from being sent? You can't.

My advice to you is to forget about trying to keep private where you go and what you do on the Internet. In fact, I'll go a step further.

Forget about keeping anything that's on your computer private once you go on-line. If you want privacy — or at least security — designate a computer for Internet use only. Use it for anything that requires a telephone line connection, but store the bulk of your data on another computer. You are vulnerable on the Internet if you don't have an impenetrable firewall. And one doesn't exist yet. Keep the systems separate. Fortunately, this is now a practical option for most people as computer prices are more affordable every day.

PLAY DETECTIVE

This exercise is one of my favorites. It provides me with countless hours of entertainment no matter where I am, on the road or at home. It makes for good practice, too. Like those times I come face-to-face with a Ms. Ramos, or her equivalent.

Your assignment is to read and make mental note of the content of every computer screen you come across during a week's time. See how easy it is to read that computer monitor at the bank or at your workplace.

Businessmen and women either on an airplane or waiting to board a flight are usually working on some important deal they're about to present or a matter they've just concluded. Of course, it's all on display right there on their computer screen. If they catch you looking, all you have to say is, "Nice screen — it's really big!" or simply, "Nice computer." You can't get someone to un-see what they have seen. Learn from this experience.

And if you're feeling a little devious and want to have some real fun (for extra credit, of course), walk into a coworker's office and ask her if you can review all her e-mail messages and their Internet site location history. (The site location history is an easily accessible file that lists Web sites that have been visited.) Watch her squirm. Wouldn't you squirm, too?

PROTECT YOURSELF

1. Treat the information in your computer the same way you would treat your most important papers. Protect it. Lock up all backup data. Use passcodes, and change them every month or so. Don't leave your computer vulnerable for someone to erase information, manipulate or change it, read, copy, or forward it. While you're away grabbing a quick bite someone could be feasting on the data in your computer!

2. Learn the difference between delete, erase, and destroy. If you have heightened confidentiality concerns, this is a critical distinction. "Delete" means not seen or easily retrievable. "Erase" means almost gone. "Destroy" means you'll be able to sleep soundly. Destroy means physically removing your hard drive, for example, smashing the beans out of it and then

throwing it out (in different containers, of course). The same distinctions apply to your backup files (disks, tapes, etc.).

3. Conduct a hardware vulnerability analysis on every computer you use. This includes personal organizers and any other electronic devices where you place information. Get to know what each cable attached to your computer is for. Make sure there's not another monitor hooked into your computer! Put a lock on all disk drives and be sure to prevent access to all ports and plugs.

4. Designate an "Internet-only computer." This computer should have nothing on it that you don't want to share with the rest of the world. This Internet-only computer has only what is necessary to surf the Internet or tap into other on-line services. Save material to a disk for transfer to your other computer. There is currently no totally effective way to guard against unwanted access unless the two hard drives are not connected in any way.

5. Demand that your Internet provider allow the option of non-credit card billing. Your Internet provider probably knows a bit too much about you. It should be your choice if you want to put your credit card information, and the plethora of information that goes with it, on the Internet. Monthly, quarterly, or yearly payments by mail should be an easy option.

6. Consider using a different name when setting up an Internet account. Or change the name currently associated with your Internet account. Simply use initials or, if you have pressing concerns, a legal alias or nickname.

7. If you charge items over the Internet, don't use your home address for the billing and delivery addresses. If you have any safety concerns, set up an alternate and safe mail location. Try to find yourself in the many Internet

people-finder directories (anywho, four11, whowhere, switch-board, bigfoot, lookupUSA) and change or erase the information about yourself.

8. Watch what you e-mail — and where you e-mail from. E-mail always identifies the sender and recipient. You just might not want to be put on an e-mail mailing list. Private or personal messages might continue after you leave a job, for example. If you have real concerns, become familiar with encryption (that codify all messages) and remailer (that hide information about the sender) programs.

9. Clear your Internet site location history. Get in the habit of erasing this file if you have any concerns about the review of where you've been roaming around on the Internet. Windows users, from your computer's main screen, open "my computer," open "control panel," open "Internet." Internet Properties will appear. Click "clear history." Then learn how to purge the cache files and folders on your computer. These files leave gorilla-size footprints.

Part Two:
MY TOOLS

HOLD STILL, THIS'LL ONLY HURT FOR A SECOND

Your secrets are my business. If the truth be told, getting information on people is part of everyone's business.

And no matter how often you vary your daily routine, how careful you are not to throw out your important papers with the household trash, how little information you actually convey when talking on the phone . . . I'm still going to find a way to ferret those secrets out.

That's what the next part of the book is all about. Not your trail — the information you unconsciously leave behind as you go about your daily business — but my tools. The methods that investigators of all types — federal, state, local, and private — use to find out what they need to know about you.

And guess what? A lot of those methods are the same ones today's con artists, scamsters, and thieves use to steal from you, methods that focus on putting you at ease, getting you to lower your guard. And while they're holding out one hand for you to shake, with the other, they're reaching into your back pocket and, ever so gently, easing out your wallet. . . .

9

THE PRETEXT

I CAN GET IT FOR YOU WHOLESALE

Among the many industries that call the Big Apple home, none is more prototypically New York than the fashion business — what, in the old days, they called the garment industry.

Walk down Seventh Avenue between Fortieth and Thirty-fourth Streets (the heart of the garment district) any day during lunchtime, and you'll see New York in microcosm. Fashionably dressed young men and women brown-bagging it in nearby Bryant Park, guys in sweatshirts sitting in the back of their delivery trucks wolfing down slices of pizza, and more traditionally attired businessmen and women on their way to a power lunch at the Royalton Hotel.

Virtually all the major players in the industry have some sort of presence in or close to this part of town. And anybody who wants to be a player in the industry needs to be located near here as well.

Back in 1992, a guy named John Andrews decided he wanted to play in the fashion business. To do so, he borrowed some money from an attorney with connections in the industry, a gentleman named Lee Holskin. Andrews took Holskin's money and connections, created his own designer label, and carved out a small niche for himself importing ties made overseas and selling them to many of the bigger retailers.

Only problem was, he never paid Holskin back the money he owed him.

Being an attorney, Holskin went to court and obtained a judgment against Andrews. After two years of trying to track down Andrews's money, Holskin came to me for help.

Holskin gave me Andrews's phone number and address — an older, ten-story office building on Eighth Avenue (the low-rent edge of the garment district). So before I started in on my usual methods, I decided to try a more direct approach.

I picked up the telephone and called Andrews.

"Import/ExportthisisMartycanIhelpyou?"

The instant I heard Marty's voice (she had a heavy New York accent, like Fran Drescher, and talked like she was getting paid by the word), an image of her formed in my mind. Fiftyish, outer-borough resident, Sears shopper, chain-smoker (and/or gum-chewer), somebody who loved to talk, somebody who loved to be helpful . . . somebody from whom I just might be able to get the information I needed without digging through trash, checking public records, or requesting any D&Bs.

"Hi," I said, as meekly as I could. "This is Terry Ardolino. I just moved in down on the third floor, and somebody said you might be able to help me find my way around the neighborhood."

"Really?" You could hear in her voice she was a bit flattered to be considered the building's expert on something. "Well, fire away, then."

"Well," I began. "Where do you guys get your coffee from?"

"We have a service that brings us the big machine and the coffee that goes with it, you know — but if you want to know the truth, I don't think much of that coffee. They got one of those Timothy's places just around the corner at Forty-first and Seventh, if you like those fancy flavored coffees, which Mr. Andrews does, and there's a Korean deli downstairs that isn't bad, but don't get it from them any time after about eleven o'clock, because they just let it sit the whole day, and. . . ."

You get the idea.

In addition to coffee, I asked Marty about the best places to get a catered lunch, where to buy office supplies . . . standard questions for the owner of a small business.

I fired off those questions one after another, like I was running down a list. Our conversation acquired a rhythm — quick question, long answer, quick question, long answer. . . .

"And where do you bank?" I asked.

"Just down the street at Marine Midland," she said. "Which I think is a good bank — I use them for my personal business as well, and I haven't had a problem. . . ."

And she was off again. I must have spent half an hour on the phone with Marty.

When I finally hung up with her, I called Lee Holskin. We obtained a court order, freezing Andrews's account at Marine Midland the next day. Holskin had his money in a week.

◻ ◻ ◻ ◻ ◻

The Merriam-Webster's dictionary defines pretext as "a purpose or motive alleged or an appearance assumed in order to cloak the real intention or state of affairs."

Pretexting is using a pretext — a cover story — to get information. When I'm looking for a pretext to begin a conversation with, I look for common ground. If I've managed to identify some of your behavioral fingerprints, I'll use one of them . . . the way I did with our comic-book-collector friend from Chapter 1.

If I don't know anything about you, I'll find another way to start the conversation — and keep it going long enough to get a feel for what it takes to lower your guard. Which, in Marty's case, wasn't much.

The pretext I use and the information I'm after don't have to be related. Notice that I started out talking to Marty about a good place to get coffee and ended up talking about where she did her banking.

Be on your guard when you're talking to strangers on the street and on the phone. There's nothing wrong with stopping to help someone who's lost, for example, but if the conversation starts to turn towards you, either redirect it back to the original topic or cut it off fast and walk away. If nothing else, maintain control of the conversation — the flow of information.

❑ ❑ ❑ ❑ ❑

Any good cover story — like any good lie — has a little bit of the truth in it. And if I can physically demonstrate to you that even part of the story I'm telling is true — say, by showing you a piece of paper that "verifies" I am who I say I am — you're all the more likely to buy the larger story I'm telling you.

Backed up by hard physical evidence, a good pretext becomes even more believable. . . .

THE COMPANY YOU KEEP

A few years back, a good friend of mine — a former European station chief for the CIA — went into business for himself. He shared his new office space with a lawyer. Within a very short span of time, my friend realized the lawyer was a crook. Not before, however, the lawyer defrauded my friend of hundreds of thousands of dollars.

But that wasn't the end of the damage he did.

The lawyer died, and dozens of other people started coming forward, claiming they'd been swindled as well. These people started harassing my friend because, after all, "You shared an office with him!"

Never mind that they weren't actually in business together. My friend was getting stuck with the lawyer's sleazy reputation. And the lawyer wasn't around anymore. How could we establish that he was the bad guy?

We had one slim chance. Though the police had classified the lawyer's death as accidental, we suspected otherwise. In fact, we suspected he'd been murdered by one of the people he'd swindled. If we could establish that, it would go a long way towards proving who was the real bad egg.

The circumstances surrounding the lawyer's death were these: On the night he died, he'd phoned his brother at about 8:30 P.M. He was in fear for his life and was leaving the country, he said. He promised to be in touch.

At 8:40 he'd phoned a car service to take him to the airport.

It was a snowy January night. The car service driver pulled into the lawyer's Westchester home a little later than expected, about 9:20 P.M.

He found the lawyer lying dead at the base of a flight of stairs, a bloodied log on one side of him, a pair of fully packed suitcases on the other.

The county medical examiner concluded the man had been carrying the log to build a fire. He'd slipped on the steps and fallen to his death. The log had flown out of his grasp and hit him on the head as he fell.

He gave no explanation as to why the man would be building a fire when he had a plane to catch.

As farfetched as the official story was, I needed the dead man's medical records to get enough evidence for the medical examiner to reverse his story.

Hospital records are not public records. To view them, you need to be related to the patient, authorized by him, or have a court order to view them.

It was easy enough to obtain identification naming me as the dead lawyer's son. . . .

"But is it really that easy?" you may well ask. Can you just print up a business card or a license (the way James Bond or Jim Rockford does), pretend to be someone else, and get admitted to places you have no business being in?

Absolutely.

With today's desktop laser printers, scanners, and computer

software, you can put together a good-looking fake ID in the comfort of your own home. Recently, my teenage cousin showed me three fake New York State driver's licenses, each one better than the last. All made by high school students.

Human nature being what it is, fake ID tends to work. People want to believe in what they see, in what you're telling them about yourself. Even a very bad fake ID will do the trick. Even an inaccurate fake ID.

Believe it or not, as I passed my fake ID over to the records clerk in the hospital, I realized that the last name was spelled wrong.

I had a momentary surge of panic. Had I just blown my friend's last chance at clearing his name?

I needn't have worried. The clerk barely glanced at the ID as she handed me a huge stack of highly confidential files.

In those files I found more than enough documentation to confirm the suspicion that all the evidence was not fully considered before the "accidental" determination. References to the force with which the hair and tissue fragments had become embedded in the log had been overlooked. We brought in the media, which was happy to publicize the medical examiner's obvious mistake. The people badgering my friend were also convinced. The guilty party had gotten his just deserts.

❑ ❑ ❑ ❑ ❑

Con artists tend to use certain kinds of fake ID. The New York City police and the city's Department for the Aging recently put out a pamphlet describing ten common scams, stings, and con games that were played on older New Yorkers. Scam #1 was con artists posing as employees of a utility company and using fake ID to gain access to the victim's home.

A healthy distrust of anyone who needs to get into your house is a good idea. Call the person's supervisor or the main office and check up on him. You may want to tell your older relatives that anyone who wants to get into their house needs to call you first.

TALKIN' THE TALK

A big part of establishing a successful pretext is using the language appropriate to your role — the terminology a travel agent, a telephone repairman, or an investment banker would use when conducting their business.

John Gallard had the language down cold.

The *New York Post* dubbed him the "World's Oldest Con Man" when, at the age of eighty-two, he scammed a group of wealthy investors (including a former United Nations undersecretary) out of millions of dollars.

I came into the case through an FBI agent I knew, who asked me to dig into Gallard's background a little.

When someone says "dig" to me, my first instinct is trash.

Unfortunately, Gallard's office was located in the same building as the Ricki Lake show, which at the time, was a very hot ticket. The show's security staff was hypersensitive to the possibility of crazed fans trying to sneak into a taping and/or harassing Ricki and her guests.

They weren't too keen on us trying to get to the maintenance area where all the trash bags were stored either.

We ended up having to go inside, into the office suites themselves, to pick up Gallard's trash. It was risky, but it was worth it. We obtained faxes and letters with completely bogus information that had gone out to other potential victims, as well as copies of communication between Gallard and his bank. We found enough to secure an indictment that ultimately led to his conviction.

I called Gallard and introduced myself by saying that I represented a few of the investors he'd dealt with. He agreed to a face-to-face meeting.

And when I say face-to-face, I mean just that. His office was the size of a broom closet, with virtually every square inch of wall covered with pictures of famous (and infamous) characters — mostly politicians, including President Reagan and then-Vice President Bush. There was room for a desk and a single rickety chair. I had to stand throughout our meeting.

Squeezing myself into the office, I told Gallard that my clients wanted to get all the facts out on the table before deciding what their next step would be.

"Next step?" Gallard asked. He had a very heavy European accent — imagine an older, smaller version of Henry Kissinger. "What kind of next step?

"Whatever lawful action needs to be taken to recover their money."

Gallard pushed back in his chair and glared up at me. "Are you implying I cheated them?" he asked.

"No, of course not," I said sarcastically. "There are just a few inconsistencies we need to clear up."

Gallard folded his hands and shook his head. "If you want my advice and even if you don't," he looked up at me and put an edge into his voice, "I think you should go away. There's nothing here for you to investigate."

I was standing over him, close to fifty years younger than he, and he couldn't have been more than five feet and a few inches tall, but he still managed to come off as threatening.

"I know people everywhere — you can ask any of them whether or not John Gallard is a thief."

And he went off on a five-minute diatribe, touting his world-wide connections to the international financial community, tossing off fifty-dollar words with such frequency that I was able to gain new insight into just how Gallard got his victims to cough up their cash so quickly.

Like I said, he had his act down cold.

That's how scam artists like Gallard work, SEC enforcement official Peter Goldstein noted after the world's oldest con man was indicted. "[They] use . . . sophisticated jargon . . . [to] convince victims that there are huge transactions normally being done by the big banks — and they can get you a piece of the action."

Gallard claimed he was a retired official of the United Bank of Switzerland. Because of his connections, he told his victims, he could offer them the opportunity to purchase a $500 million bank note for $425 million for a $250,000 up-front fee.

(I later learned that Gallard was so smooth, so polished, so confident and forceful, that one victim in San Francisco and his attorney/partner in London both wired him $250K within hours of talking to him.)

Once he had his victim's money, Gallard made up another story, one that had to do with bureaucratic red tape that caused the investors to forfeit their deposit.

Then he offered his victims the chance to salvage the money by helping them resell the forfeited note to other investors.

Gallard ended his speech to me by saying, "I never guaranteed them anything. I made it clear I was strictly acting as their financial advisor."

"Of course," I said. I pointed at the picture of Reagan. "You were his financial advisor too, I assume?"

Gallard glared at me again.

"And what celestial authority empowered you to offer a half-billion dollars' worth of Mormon Bonds as security to obtain bank loans?" I asked. "Did God say you could do that? I'm sure the Mormon Church didn't give you the O.K."

"Are you making fun of me?" he asked.

I smiled. "Well, we'll certainly check into everything," I said. "I have a call in to God."

"Listen to me very carefully," he said. "I'm going to f***ing kill you."

"If you had a habit of keeping promises, I'd be concerned. Trust me, I won't lose any sleep tonight."

A day later, I received notice that he'd filed a complaint against me with the cops.

When I wasn't arrested, he filed another complaint, accusing me of paying them off.

When that didn't work, he sued me (as well as President Clinton and Vice President Gore, among others) in a multibillion-dollar lawsuit.

It really got to be a running joke, especially when I discovered that the lawyer Gallard initially hired, a guy named George Nash, had in fact been disbarred years earlier.

Later on, Gallard was legally represented by an even bigger boob — himself — in his unsuccessful attempt to prevent the SEC from indicting and convicting him of securities fraud.

A FORMAL APPROACH

"I got the authorization right here," I said. I turned the clipboard I was carrying around so Richard Smyth could read the form for himself.

"See?"

Smyth glanced down at the form, then back up at me. "Just make it quick. I have to go out," he said.

I nodded, glancing at the moving boxes stacked near the door. Smyth was not only going out soon, he was leaving town — permanently — in a few days.

Smyth had been feeling a little heat since his friend, the mayor of Waterbury, Connecticut, had been indicted on bribery charges. Everyone had considered Smyth and the mayor inseparable and the best of friends. To make matters more pressing, another friend of Smyth's and the mayor's committed suicide.

Sheila, a quick, no-nonsense investigator, and I were brought up from Washington to assist on the case. Information had been obtained indicating that Smyth might be trying to leave town before he, too, got indicted. Sheila and I were to keep an eye on the good Mr. Smyth.

We were on a break — eating lunch at a restaurant near our subject's rented home — when Sheila came up with the strategy that eventually worked. As we walked into the restaurant, she reached into a large glass bowl on the hostess counter, and fished out a handful of variously colored business cards.

"Having trouble meeting men?" I asked.

A sharp look but no answer.

After we'd been led to our table, she neatly arranged the business cards. While I studied the menu, she reviewed her catch.

"Hmmm, lawyer, lawyer, doctor, computer consultant, roto-router, lawyer.

"There's either too many lawyers around here or they eat at this restaurant too much," I said as I put my menu down on the table.

"Ah. Here we go," Sheila said.

"Did you find a guy?" I asked.

"As you know, I'm happily married, but you, my friend, are . . . are . . . a painting contractor." She placed the business card before me: "Matt Hillis Contracting — for all your plastering and painting needs."

It took less than five minutes that evening to print up the almighty form that would direct me to conduct a painting appraisal on the apartment Richard Smyth was vacating.

A few quick doodles about room size and quantity of paint brought me back near Smyth's front door within ten minutes. He had been watching me like a hawk.

"Hey, good luck with the move. I hate moving — bad back. Where are you headed?"

"Yeah, thanks, uh, Charlotte. See ya."

Maybe, I thought. But even if you don't see me, I'll be seeing you — in Charlotte. He had confirmed verbally what I had already read off a box ready to be mailed: his new address in Charlotte, North Carolina.

❏ ❏ ❏ ❏ ❏

Remember how easy it is to create fake ID? The same goes for those official-looking forms, like the one I showed Richard Smyth. Now, more than ever, you can't automatically believe what you read. Take the time to verify all information. Most pretexts divert the power, direction, or authority to a nonpresent, and usually nonexistent, individual. ("Well, that's what I was told to do by my boss.") Check everything. Then recheck it.

PLAY DETECTIVE

You need to do the following live — in person. No hiding behind a telephone (that will come in the next chapter).

You are to assume someone else's identity. Just borrow one for a short period of time: another coworker's, a repairman's, a salesperson's, a taxi driver's.

The next time your friend, coworker, or relative calls you by name (in person, remember), politely correct them with your new name. ("I'm sorry, you're mistaken. I'm Matt Hillis.") As they give you a weird look and contemplate having you committed, repeat your name and offer your occupation ("Matt Hillis, the painting contractor"). Now, and this is the fun part, state why you are there and then just ramble on about how hard a day you're having, how big a job this is going to be, etc. Interject some off-the-wall questions. Be sure to flick your eyes about the room.

"I'm here for the estimate, to paint the place. What a mess. When was the last time this was painted? Those cracks are going to be a big problem. Do you know if they used oil or latex? A lotta work, a lotta work. Big job, this is going to be a big job. Which room do you think I should paint first? Are they predicting rain today?"

Observe how quickly you can get your target here into playing along.

That's how easy it is to pretext someone. That's how easily someone can pretext you. Learn from this experience. How many times each day do you play out encounters similar to this one?

PROTECT YOURSELF

1. **Practice your verbal defenses — now.** Don't wait until you're off guard and unprepared. Here are some techniques to rehearse:

a) Answer questions with a question — scamsters hate this.

b) Deflect questions with a well-rehearsed line: "I don't want to talk about that now," "I was told not to discuss that," "I don't know much about that; I'm not the person you should be talking to." Keep repeating the same answer until they hang up on you or walk away.

c) Practice saying "No," even if it's not a particularly appropriate response.

d) Answer only the question being asked. Provide no further information or comment. Listen to lawyers. They've been trained to do just that.

2. **Establish specific guidelines for your family and coworkers about when and to whom they should give out information.** Most people provide too much information because they just aren't prepared. Be specific. Say, "Don't give out any information about such-and-such without talking to me first." "You can speak to my wife about anything, just as if you're talking to me." Ask hypothetical questions. For example, "How would you respond if someone asked you for my phone number/the bank I use/where I work/when I'll be home?" People want to be guided and directed in this area. And practice, practice, practice. Pay special attention to children and the elderly. Ask others how you should respond to similar inquiries made about them.

3. **Make believe people who could potentially release information about you (your banker, your neighbor, your receptionist, etc.) are your press agents.** What information do you want them giving out? Find out if your bank account has these three security check points: a passcode that's necessary to receive any information, a list of items approved to be given out by telephone, and a list of information only to be released upon written request.

4. **Question authority: Double-check documents and employee IDs.** If someone gives you a call (your banker, law

enforcement, a friend's friend) and you don't know the person or can't recognize his voice, don't give out any information. Politely ask him where he is calling from and get his telephone number so you can call back. Verify the number by calling directory assistance or consulting your records. Call the number you know to be that company's telephone number, not the one provided for you. Also, confirm written documentation. Prove it isn't fake.

In the Gallard matter, people should have called bankers and previous clients and then checked from another angle, for example, public records. That "previous satisfied client" just might be a relative, friend, or partner in crime. Most government agencies (the SEC, licensing departments, etc.) can help. Simply call and ask, "How can I check a license, an employee, etc.?"

5. Carefully examine the ID of any utility workers who come to your house. Assume that ID is false until you can be convinced otherwise. Check with employee supervisors and verify the employee's physical description if you have any concerns. Also, ask your utility company to install outside meters.

6. Use extra caution with newspaper ads and for-sale signs. Obviously, if you are selling something or advertising your services, you're more likely to be receptive, friendly, and open to a verbal crowbar. Be prepared.

7. Resist responding to the illusion of urgency. The best and most damaging pretexts pounce for the kill the moment you're responding to an emergency or some other highly emotionally charged atmosphere. Be careful if you hear, for example, "Congratulations, you've won . . ." or "This is Inspector Wolfe from the bank fraud department. . . ."

8. Resist the urge NOT to check. Many people might not check out a situation thoroughly because they're convinced they need to cover for someone or because they are tempted to do

something that may be sneaky, sleazy, or improper. For example, buying a "new" item (TV, VCR, etc.) at a fraction of the actual cost from someone they don't know is both a temptation and a moral dilemma perhaps. Remember the attitude of "Ahhh, I don't want to know" can be used against you. Gather and review the facts. Then decide which course of action to take.

9. Be a good neighbor. Discuss with neighbors (and neighboring businesses) how inquiries should be handled or to whom they should be referred. Keep your eyes open and, in a nice way, question people and events. Say, "Hi, we all keep an eye on each other around here. What are you doing? What's going on?"

10

EAVESDROPPING AND PHONE SCAMS

LET THAT BE A LESSON TO YOU

A few years ago, I was walking down Sixth Avenue in midtown Manhattan when my beeper went off. It was an ex-federal agent and friend of mine, who was in the middle of working a particularly juicy case — Larry King's umpteenth ugly divorce.

The radio/television personality was in from Washington that night, staying at a swanky midtown hotel. My friend, who was working for King's then-wife, wanted me to help find out the identity of King's new girlfriend. For some unknown reason it was a closely guarded secret. My friend had a few associates on the Amtrak Metroliner following King and his unidentified girlfriend.

They had broadcast *Larry King Live* in New York that evening and got to bed pretty late. But early the next morning, King checked out of the hotel, the girlfriend in tow. Right away, I went to work. The only hope I had was that Larry's girlfriend had used the telephone to call her friends or relatives or to check her home answering machine.

My friend was skeptical about my flimsy theory. I was guardedly hopeful.

"Hell, if I was spending the night with Larry King in a fancy hotel in New York, I'd probably phone a few friends and tell them."

My friend starts laughing.

"Uh, maybe that didn't come out the way I had intended," I said quietly.

I called the hotel's accounting department, pretending to be the travel coordinator from King's Washington, D.C. offices.

After introducing myself, I launched into my spiel. "Look, I'm calling because the New York office paid for this [the hotel] directly, and they shouldn't have. Our department always takes care of these things. You people know this. Mr. Powers is very upset about this. We're going to have to do a transfer. I need you to fax me over a copy of the entire hotel bill right away."

(Note that at no time during this conversation did I say please.)

Faced with the urgency in my voice, the official-sounding nature of my request, and her own inclination to believe what she was hearing, she faxed a copy of the bill to an associate of mine waiting at a public fax service in Washington. The bill included a detailed listing of every phone call that had been made from King's suite of rooms.

Whoops — every long distance call. Not the local ones.

I had to call back again.

"Hi. Listen, can you help me out here? Powers wants full documentation. You didn't include detailed itemization of the local phone charges. Can you send that over right away?"

She sends the local calls over. Great.

Now my friend is getting greedy. He wants to know to which credit card the room was charged, to see if Larry was using a joint marital credit card account. Although this request would contradict my previous conversations, I had to call back and try. I wasn't quite sure how I was going to tiptoe through that minefield, but I figured I'd wing it.

But this time, the second the woman comes on the line, her

attitude is very different.

"I just called your Washington office," she says. "They've never heard of you."

"Well," I say. "That's odd."

"I shouldn't have sent any of that information over to you." She's understandably upset — and a little panicked that she screwed up. "I shouldn't have faxed you anything."

She must have repeated those same words a dozen times: "I shouldn't have sent you any of that information. I shouldn't have sent you any of that information. I shouldn't have sent you any of that information. . . ."

After a while, it started to sound like a mantra.

Finally, she finished. The line was silent; she was waiting for me to say something, perhaps apologize.

She repeated the words one final time: "I shouldn't have sent you anything."

"Well," I said. "Let that be a lesson to you."

Let that be a lesson to you, too.

Beware the telephone's magical powers. With a telephone, a con artist can elicit sympathy, help, and cold hard cash from people who wouldn't give him the time of day under other circumstances. The properly trained scamster can enter the most secure environment on the planet — any home, any office.

The telephone is the perfect pretexting tool. All the visual and contextual clues that might otherwise warn you of a person's bad intentions are eliminated. All you hear is a voice.

The telephone's power is virtually absolute.

The bell rings, most of us answer and obey.

Want proof of how deeply ingrained our Pavlovian behavior is? This has assuredly happened to you: You're standing in line at a store waiting to be helped when the phone rings. The clerk answers and starts to help the person on the phone (who didn't even roll out of bed yet!), while asking you, the schmuck who hoofed it to this place, who's been waiting and waiting, to hold on a minute.

(The caller should be told, "I have forty-three people in line here. You are now number forty-four. I'm going to put the phone down on the counter and then pick it up and help you after I've helped person number forty-three — it'll be about an hour." But don't hold your breath. This won't be happening anytime soon.)

Telemarketers and telephone con artists are all thoroughly trained to overcome your objections to their pitch. They practice all day long. You — their intended victim — should practice also.

Let's start with how you answer the phone. When you pick up the receiver, you should take charge of the conversation immediately.

Let the caller know that you're a busy person, with no time to waste.

How? With your tone of voice.

When people hear you say "Hello?" — with a rising inflection at the end of the word they assume that means you are now at their disposal.

I tend to say "good afternoon," "good morning," or "good evening," depending on the time of day, obviously — in a very neutral, matter-of-fact tone. From there I can segue into whatever response is appropriate.

Whatever you say, your tone of voice should clearly announce, "I'm not a potential victim."

You should also practice hanging up the phone.

Say, "Have a nice day. Goodbye." Don't wait for a response, just hang up. Use language you feel comfortable with, and rehearse the lines. For example:

- "Please put your offer in writing and mail it to me. I have to go."
- "I'm not interested, thank you."
- "I have no money . . . and don't expect any anytime soon."
- "I've never bought anything by telephone, and never will."

Or simply,

- "No. Goodbye."

I'm sure you can think up others.

The important thing is to say the line, and then hang up. Right away. Don't wait for their response, don't wait to see how they react, and don't feel bad about cutting them off. In case you didn't notice, they invaded your privacy.

It is important to get off the phone as quickly as possible. Believe me, all these solicitors have been handed responses to every conceivable objection you could make (your individual pattern). If they get their foot in the door, there is a good chance that they will eventually succeed. End the call when you want to — not when they've finished their pitch.

Practice, practice, practice — with your friends, your coworkers, and your family, especially your elderly relatives and your children.

❏ ❏ ❏ ❏ ❏

Con artists love the telephone. Whether they're trying to sell you vacation shares at a nonexistent resort, solicit money for a bogus charity, or get an advance for a nonexistent service they promise to provide, they spend a lot of time glued to one end of Alexander Graham Bell's famous invention.

But technology has come a long way since Bell first invented the phone, and with the advent of cellular telephones, a whole new world has opened up for con artists. . . .

PHONE CLONES

The term is "cloning," and I'm not talking about creating identical twins.

Cloning, in this instance, involves the theft of the technology behind your cell phone service — the duplication of both your cellular phone number and something called an ESN number. The ESN number is a unique identifier assigned to your actual telephone. Those two numbers together allow for telephone calls to be made.

Well, guess what?

Some crooks figured out they could snatch those two sets of numbers from the air (again, using an inexpensive scanner), reprogram them into any other cell phone, and make calls. To the company providing your service — and sending the bill — it looks like you made those calls.

It's the equivalent of a crook's coming to your front door and your handing them your cordless phone. The crook can call wherever he wants himself, or he can stand on the corner and let a "customer" call his friends in Peru for five dollars.

Washington Heights, New York, happens to be the cloning capital of the world. Crooks set up shop in apartments overlooking the George Washington Bridge. The endless parade of cell phone users passing over the bridge (often stuck in slow-moving traffic) provides easy pickings.

A couple of years ago, the cloning problem became so widespread that cellular telephone companies added another layer to their security measures by requiring security codes on all cellular calls. It didn't take long for the crooks to figure a way around them, either.

Today's newest technology, digital cellular phones, has digital safeguards. You can bet the crooks will find a way around them, too. As the cat-and-mouse game continues, make sure you don't become a victim.

❑ ❑ ❑ ❑ ❑

Con artists are also in on the kind of eavesdropping games our friend "Gene Hackman" ran back in Chapter 5 to catch "Carmen Electra."

In the past, most assignments for eavesdropping began with an objective, some sort of issue that needed to be explored. Once you had identified the problem and the players, you started collecting information. You began attempting to uncover the truth and gather all the facts.

But today's high-tech eavesdroppers start by collecting large amounts of information from your cellular telephone conversations — any information — and then finding someone who will pay for it. A juicy morsel about a celebrity can be sold to the *National Enquirer* or the *Globe*. A small bit of information can reap piles of cash from an opponent in a nasty legal battle. A five-second conversation about a large corporation can have windfall rewards from an appreciative stockbroker.

Don't think you're safe in your car, either; someone in that BMW behind you could be listening in.

All he needs to do is find the frequency you're transmitting on — using the same kind of inexpensive scanner we talked about in Chapter 5 — and he can listen in on your every word. (Yes, that frequency changes as you travel from one cell site to another, but all the eavesdropper needs to do is rescan for your new frequency.)

❑ ❑ ❑ ❑ ❑

You might think it would be harder to monitor a standard telephone conversation. You'd be wrong.

Tying into the physical wires that lead to your phone (wiretapping) is a piece of cake for any qualified operative. And if you can connect two wires together, you're qualified.

During one investigation, I discovered that a man wanted by the FBI had holed up in a motel on Long Island, New York. As important as capturing him was finding out where his accomplices were — which meant listening in on his phone.

I was able to get the room next to his. At midnight, I left my room for the lobby, where I gave the desk clerk a handful of unimportant papers to fax. I tipped him twenty bucks, and headed out for a cup of coffee.

When I came back, I asked for a copy of my bill — giving the clerk the fugitive's room number. The copy he gave me contained a record of every telephone number the fugitive had called.

I found nothing of use.

Returning to my room, I tried monitoring the fugitive through the wall. I ended up having to take the wall apart, right down to the molding, to access the phone wire.

When guile fails, brute force must do.

Or ingenuity.

Listen to this. Let's say I know you usually answer the phone on the second ring when you're at work. I know your partner in crime, who works out of his home, answers on the fourth or fifth ring. I call the slower answerer first on a two-line telephone. Then, with a little practice — and a little bit of luck — I conference the quicker answerer. They both say "hello" at about the same time. There is usually a half-second of confusion — both people saying hello to each other at the same time. But the sound of each other's voice and the need to relay some sort of thought dispels any concern. They proceed to have a conversation — and you get to hear the whole thing!

Nowadays, with people used to the clicks, static, and frequent disconnections that accompany cellular and cordless phone reception, this trick has become even easier to pull off.

The recent advances in telecommunications technologies — call forwarding, caller ID, *69, etc. — offer investigators and con artists alike a whole new bag of tools to play with.

Take the granddaddy of all the features referred to above — the redial button, which we discussed briefly back in Chapter 5. How could one be used against you?

An attorney, Chris Lenfeston, once asked me to join him on a late-night visit to a client's office. The attorney felt that his client, Mark Kenny, wasn't being totally honest with him and wanted me to knock (figuratively, of course) some sense into him.

The situation, in a nutshell, was this. Mark suspected his business partner, Andy, of cheating him. He wanted the attorney to catch the partner at it. But once we sat down with Mark in his office, it became obvious to me as well that Mark was only telling the attorney part of the story — the part he thought his lawyer needed to know.

"I need more details, more background. How can I help you if you're not totally honest with me?" Chris pleaded. There was just more double-talk from Mark. After a few minutes of back-and-forth, Mark turned to me.

"Why don't you take a look around? See if you can find anything?" he asked.

"What am I supposed to be looking for?" I asked, immediately suspecting that he had planted something for me to discover. As he pointed to the office down the hall I almost asked him, "Well, I'm sure you checked it. I bet you know what I'll find." But I kept my mouth shut and disappeared into Andy's office.

As I sat in Andy's four-hundred-dollar desk chair, admiring the lavish furnishings, I debated whether or not to even look for what I was supposed to find. Then I got a better idea.

I reached for the phone and dialed a number I knew very well. Before anyone could answer, I hung up and headed out the door. I met Chris and Mark in the hallway. "I need to ask you about something in your partner's office," I said. As the three of us re-entered the room I'd just left, I pointed to a large, locked file cabinet in the corner, as if I had discovered a hidden treasure.

"Do we know what's in there?" I asked.

"I'm not worried about what's in the file cabinet — I know what's in the file cabinet!" Mark exclaimed. He was annoyed I hadn't found what I was supposed to have found, I supposed.

I pointed to the telephone. "Does he have speed-dial or redial — or whatever it's called? It'd be nice to see who he calls." Mark's eyes widened. As I started talking about the file cabinet again, he walked over to the phone, pushed the speakerphone and hit redial. The three of us stared at the phone as a voice squawked, "FBI."

I had every intention of being the person to push the redial button. He just beat me to it.

After his initial shock — and a short blast of anger — Mark was suddenly quite forthcoming with a much more detailed picture of the operation he and his partner had been running together. He was clearly petrified that his partner, Andy, had beaten him by getting to "the feds" before he did.

It turned out Mark and Andy had been evading taxes and

selling "opportunities" to people on nonexistent coal mining businesses.

The point is not to rely too much on what technology tells you. Always take it a step further. Check the person's intentions.

❑ ❑ ❑ ❑ ❑

A few years ago, I received a phone call at three in the morning from an old friend of mine. She was totally distraught.

"Janey, what happened?" I asked.

She explained that she had just spent the last three hours at the police station. Her ex-husband had filed a complaint against her for harassment — the second such complaint her ex had filed. After the first, a judge had ordered her not to telephone her ex again, threatening her with jail time if she violated the order. Which she'd apparently just done.

This did not sound like the Janey I knew.

I got to Janey's home a little before 4 A.M. to find her sobbing in her sister's arms. She told me what had happened in court after the husband's first complaint. The prosecutor had presented her telephone records as evidence that she had, in fact, telephoned the ex-husband. On the stand she admitted to being the only person in the home on the night in question. This wasn't good. To make matters worse, Janey made a horrible witness because she became quite irate when no one would believe her. She showed me a copy of the trial transcript, where the judge had told her, "Miss, you stated that you were the only person home and that, as you had the alarm set, no one entered the premises. We have all reviewed the records from the telephone company indicating that calls were placed from your home to the complainant's home on the night in question. You can't explain how the calls got on your phone bill. The officer testified that he examined the victim's caller ID and witnessed your telephone number along with the dates and times of those calls. I do not believe that you are telling the truth. I think you are a troubled young woman. I find you guilty. Sentencing, two weeks from today. Next case."

Tonight again, like the first time, Janey swore she didn't call him. I wanted so much to believe her. In the many years we had known each other, I had always marveled at her honesty — even when she did dumb things, she was never evasive in any way.

Could she be telling the truth in this case, too?

It was time to call in help — a group of the most creative minds imaginable — friends and associates from every walk of life. Janey knew what I meant when I told her, "I'm calling the Group. I need a few days."

A few days passed. Joe, one of the more brilliant members of the group, and I were walking around the house for the umpteenth time chanting, "How would we do it? How the hell would we do it?"

Suddenly Joe stopped walking.

"A lineman's phone?" he asked.

I smiled. "A lineman's phone."

A lineman's phone is the phone repairman's telephone set with the two alligator clips — the clips that can be attached to just about any phone wire anywhere, including the wires that run down the outside of almost every home.

We examined Janey's phone wires and found very tiny holes where her ex must have attached the clips. He had simply walked up to the side of the house late at night and connected into her telephone line. Then he dialed his own number and let his answering machine pick up so the call would register as having been completed.

We knew how he did it. Now we had to catch him in the act.

The following Saturday night (I suppose he picked that night because he thought it would be harder to get ahold of her lawyer, harder to post bail, no judge until Monday, etc.), I watched the husband squeeze through the hedges around Janey's house to make his midnight call. My only regret was not having a bunch of attack dogs waiting. The videotape would have to do.

Remember, all these new telephone features (call forwarding, call return, redial, caller ID, three-way calling, etc.) are nice to have, but view them with suspicion. They all can be used to create an illusion.

And sometimes you don't even have to try. . . .

A BORING CONVERSATION

Baton Rouge, Louisiana, attorney Jim Boren learned the hard way that you really need to pay attention to simple telephone technology. He thought a telephone conference call with a few people who had just questioned his knowledge of simple legal principles had been disconnected. These people had recently wired him seventy thousand dollars. But before his office properly disconnected the telephone lines, he was overheard referring to the people who sent him the money as "those bastards." It turned out to be a very costly call.

❏ ❏ ❏ ❏ ❏

Remarkably, the same little telephone games we all played as adolescents can be used by information gatherers and scamsters. Do you lower your guard when someone appears very young, very old, or challenged in some way? Keep the conversation appropriate, controlled, and focused. Be determined *not* to answer any questions until you are in control of the content of the telephone conversation. Your having control over a conversation usually involves *you* asking questions! Answer a question with a question as a way to harness an aggressive caller's techniques and get satisfactory answers to any concerns you might have. For a question like, "Is Vicki home?" it's as simple as asking, "Who's calling, please?" or as aggressive as responding, "Please tell me why you need that information."

LET YOUR FINGERS DO THE TALKING

If you're ever in Manhattan and you've got a few spare minutes, head on over to the historic Murray Hill district, just east of the Empire State Building. Stop at the corner of Thirty-fourth Street and Park Avenue. On the northwest corner of the intersection, you'll see two pay phones, mounted back-to-back next to the curb.

Assume for the sake of argument that one of those pay phones isn't working. Further assume that two garbage bags are stacked one on top of the other directly next to the working phone, so that there's only one place you can conceivably stand — slightly to the side, leaning in — if you need to make an outgoing call.

And now (again, for the sake of argument) assume that there's a car parked next to the pay phone, and in the back seat of that car is a large box, which is almost — but not quite — completely sealed. There's just enough room for the lens of a miniature video camera to peek through — and that zoom lens is trained on the keypad of the working pay phone.

Were all of the above true, that video camera would be able to capture whatever numbers were punched in on the phone keypad, local or long-distance calls, 800 numbers, directory assistance, etc.

This might even be a good way to get someone's voicemail code — or the calling card number they use to bill their long distance calls to their home phone.

I witnessed this very same technique used on a deserving target a few years back. While being followed, he was beeped to his home telephone, just as he neared the two telephones. His travel route had been established, and we were waiting for him to use the only working phone.

So if you get the feeling all eyes are on you when you make a call out on the street, they very well may be. In these days of passwords and security codes, a thief who can access one or more of your PINs can find out vital information about you and/or run up several thousand dollars' worth of calls. You'll never know it's being done, until your phone bill shows up.

When you push buttons on a telephone touch pad in public, you can foil prying eyes very easily. Those eyes can only see what numbers you appear to be pushing. You are the only one who can feel the touch and subsequent depression of each number.

Practice a bit. It's really quite easy. For example, if you are dialing the code 1-2-3-4-5, push the 1 and 2 buttons, touch the 9 and 8 keys (lightly touch, without depressing), then depress the 3, 4, and 5 buttons. Whether those nosy people are looking or videotaping, they won't get too far.

If you don't have your calling card information memorized, you must guard against others reading it. I often see people holding their calling card up so they can read it. Or they place the card on top of the phone or on the small table base. This is a big mistake. That card can either be reproduced or charged to the limit by fraudsters in an extremely short period of time.

Once, while waiting for a flight at La Guardia Airport, I stood at a bank of telephones and overheard one very loud, self-important, middle-aged guy constantly barking his telephone calling card number to an operator. I made note of the calling card number — his home telephone number with a four-digit PIN. I called his home answering machine (no, I didn't bill the call to his card) and left a message reciting his calling card information and advising him that if he weren't more careful he'd probably be getting a five-thousand-dollar phone bill courtesy of the scamsters that roam around airports and train stations in search of nitwits like him.

❑ ❑ ❑ ❑ ❑

Access codes (PINs, security codes, remote codes, etc.) — for voicemail boxes, answering machines, what have you — are safety barriers. But remember, these codes are made to be broken. Usually, and preferably, by you. But sometimes the codes are easily used by those not authorized by you who have just a little bit of patience and perseverance.

Denied a legal wiretap on one case I was working on, we

decided to obtain the security code for our target's answering machine. With no other options available to us, we started guessing. When guessing didn't work we simply started at square one: Zero. Double-zero. Zero one. Zero two. Zero three . . . and so on.

After four ten-hour days, we had it. 6091. (Luckily, it was a four-digit number. A five-digit one might have taken us another few weeks.)

Answering machine codes should be changed periodically, especially if you are concerned about your privacy. I change mine at least once a month, using a system tied to the calendar. (See code-changing tips in Chapter 11.)

And check your outgoing message announcement at least every month or so. I've known people bent on causing trouble to change outgoing messages to advise callers of specific information or to divert callers to another number.

Make sure the volume on your answering machine is always set low, so no one can listen in. All the high-tech phone security defenses in the world can't prevent a person standing outside from listening as someone leaves a message or you play your messages back. I have spent hours just sitting in a hallway listening to messages left on loud answering machines.

PLAY DETECTIVE

This might sound sleazy but there's an important lesson to be learned here. Besides, you've done worse. Try to break an answering machine or voicemail access code. Don't try this on anyone you know. It's really not nice. Try different systems, enter commands: zero, the * or # buttons. Then enter 1-2-3-4-5-6-7-8-9-10. Then the fun begins: 00-01-02-03, and so on.

I hope you will experience two important revelations before you actually break the code: one, if someone is determined, they can probably break your code; and two, it's probably easier to accomplish than you thought.

PROTECT YOURSELF

1. Be assertive on the telephone. Other than calls you welcome, every call is a potential violator of your privacy. Ask the questions you want, take control of the conversation when you want, hang up when you want.

2. Don't respond to questions that make you uncomfortable. Have a planned response or simply be silent. Practice with friends and family. When in doubt, answer a question with a question. Say, "I don't know. What do you think?" Shut them down with the old favorite: "No, thank you" (and just keep repeating it). If pushed, "I have to go now." And then hang up.

3. Practice pushing numbers on the telephone keypad when you're entering a code in public. Assume that you are being watched and provide misinformation by lightly touching some numbers you don't actually press.

4. Buy a phone recorder that records everything each time the line is answered. You'll hear if anyone attempts to break your code or play back your messages. Any Radio Shack will be able to provide you with an economical telephone recorder.

5. Change your answering machine/voicemail codes periodically. Are you still using the code that you used three boyfriends ago? Try to change your access code every month or so, but be sure to make code changes when the people in your life change. Access codes should be a minimum of four digits.

6. Don't be fooled by the proper-sounding background noise. The clicking of a computer keyboard doesn't guarantee that the call is from your bank or credit card company.

I could be lying on a lounge chair with a keyboard (not attached to anything) on my lap, typing away, making the right noises, "Mrs. Greene. Tyler James here. I'm trying to process your application and I need to go over some of the details with you. . . ." When in doubt, verify and call them back.

11

ROBBING YOUR IDENTITY

THE RIGHT MAN FOR THE JOB

I spent five hundred dollars on the suit.

Another fifty on the haircut.

And to make sure I came off as the ideal candidate for the job . . .

I borrowed someone's identity.

"Kevin!" John Bohrman, the gentleman behind the desk, stood and waved me into his office. "Thanks for coming in to see us again."

"My pleasure," I said. "I'm hoping to be part of the team."

"Well, we're all impressed so far," Bohrman said. "This should be your final interview."

"Good," I replied, and meant it. The federal government had been trying for months to get someone inside Bohrman's company — the Paradigm Group, formerly known as the Caserta Group (CGI). I was the first person to have made it this far, to a second interview with the boss himself.

Paradigm was located in Manhasset, a Long Island suburb

about forty-five minutes outside of New York City. The company was housed in a four-story office building. Also housed in that building was another company that Peter Caserta, Bohrman's father-in-law, had ties to: Spectrum Technologies.

"Have a seat," Bohrman said, waving me into a gray, cushioned chair in front of his desk. He picked up a piece of paper on his desk and glanced over it.

I'd recognize that paper anywhere: my resume.

I'd spent so much time crafting that document, I think I could have quoted it to him line for line.

The resume wasn't exactly mine, of course. Most of the items on it belonged to one Kevin McNamara, whose social security number, driver's license information, school records, old addresses, and employment history I'd borrowed (at the government's request) in order to aid the investigation of Paradigm.

The government had received several complaints from companies that had been ripped off by Bohrman and his associates. So when Paradigm ran an ad for a telephone solicitor in the *New York Times*, ten federal agents applied for the position.

None was called in for an interview.

After the government's initial failure to get past Paradigm's background checkers, we decided my history — at least, the history I gave them — needed to be spotless.

My first step had been to have an associate go to the local colleges and comb through copies of their old school yearbooks. Her job was to find a guy who looked somewhat like me and was approximately the same age. She came back with one Kevin McNamara, a 1987 graduate of Columbia University in New York, who could have passed for my brother. The fact that our names were so similar was a bonus.

With the government's assistance, I spent the next day constructing my life.

All I had to add to the records we obtained was a recent move to account for my new telephone number and new address; my pending "divorce" explained that nicely.

By the time we'd finished putting together my life as Kevin

McNamara, I felt I'd lived it, which was critical. One hesitant reply to questions about my history and I'd lose my chance at the job.

"I see you've had extensive telephone sales experience," Bohrman said. "That's very important. Results are essential here."

Bohrman went on to say that Paradigm was a high-pressure environment. My job would be not only to make the initial contact and sales presentation to the companies I would call, but to follow up with them repeatedly, if necessary. In addition to my commission, I would draw a weekly salary.

"That sounds good to me," I told him. "All I need is the opportunity to show you what I can do."

"Now I have to ask you this, Kevin." Bohrman leaned forward in his chair. "Have you ever worked for the police?"

I sat back in my chair.

Truthfully, I'd been expecting a question like this. The stench of something rotten had begun to gather around Paradigm — a negative article about the company had recently appeared in one of the New York papers, and there were rumors (very accurate ones, obviously) about the government looking into the company's operations. I'd have been surprised if Bohrman wasn't concerned.

I don't know what he thought he would gain by coming right out and asking me if I was a cop. He'd obviously watched too many police shows on television, where the law always came clean when confronted with a direct question.

I wasn't operating by those rules.

"Okay, hold on a minute," I said. "If there's anything improper going on here, I don't want the job. Not with being in the middle of a divorce and all."

"Nothing illegal . . . improper," Bohrman assured me. "We've just had some problems with disgruntled employees."

I assured him I'd never been a cop, which was technically the truth.

"Well, Kevin," Bohrman said, rising from his desk and extending his hand. "Welcome to Paradigm."

The next morning, I began my training session. This session consisted of reading a few paragraph-long sales pitches and then observing other "sales associates." Our telephone targets brought up some very good questions. But Paradigm had scripted some incredible responses that not only sounded great but actually made sense.

I was impressed by the other sales associates, who ranged in age from about nineteen to forty. I began making sales calls for the company that very day, sharing a small office with another phone solicitor.

But I soon discovered that the bosses didn't entirely trust me.

Every time I went to the bathroom, my desk was searched.

When I left my desk, I arranged the flap on my suit jacket a certain way. When I returned, it was always moved. The government let me know that they (my new employers) were not only monitoring my work but all my telephone calls as well.

I always kept the map I was making of the premises on my person, in my underwear, in fact. This map, essential for the day of the raid, noted the location of every office in Paradigm, every trash can, filing cabinet, chair, telephone, etc. This way, on the day of the raid, important evidence could be immediately secured. And of course, during my daily routine, I was nailing down the details of exactly how Paradigm's scam worked.

We, the telephone solicitors, were given a list of companies that were pulling in a minimum of thirty million dollars per year. The thirty-second sales pitch touted Paradigm — "we're in business to help companies like yours" — and its ability to secure ten or twenty million dollars in seed capital for the business owner.

This pitch, by the way, had instant credibility because each solicitor made sure to mention Paradigm's close relationship to Peter Caserta and Spectrum Technologies — whose new chairman was John Sculley, from Apple Computer. Once Sculley's name was dropped, business owners fell all over themselves to get into business with Paradigm.

And, this is very important, we were not B.S.ing folks ninety-eight years old. We were bamboozling successful young and middle-aged businessmen and women who ran their own companies. We concentrated on small to medium-size technology-based companies

— companies that were into anything having to do with computers and the then-current explosion in cellular phone technology. But the truth of the matter was, no matter what business they were in, if the company was grossing thirty to forty million a year, we were more than happy to take fifty thousand dollars from them.

Once we had their attention it was important to create urgency: We'd have to move quickly. "Our board is meeting the day after tomorrow and I'd like your company to be one of the few I'm going to present." You could just hear them thinking that *their* company's financing plan would be presented to John Sculley himself in a short forty-eight hours. "You could wire just half of the fifty thousand tomorrow and the balance next week, if that would help you out."

This was the money the target company needed to advance as the "due diligence" fee to Paradigm to pay for the investigation needed to demonstrate to potential investors the company's soundness and to put all the papers in order.

Needless to say, this money disappeared into Paradigm's pockets and was never seen again. Nor did any of the potential investors Paradigm touted ever appear.

On March 23, 1994, based on the information I gathered during my tenure at Paradigm, a dozen federal agents armed with a search warrant burst into the premises at 1615 Northern Boulevard in Manhasset. As Paradigm's office was secured and we employees detained and processed, agents began seizing enough paper to fill the seven-ton truck parked outside.

Bohrman and his associates were convicted of wire and mail fraud and sent to prison.

❑ ❑ ❑ ❑ ❑

Identity theft is one of the country's fastest-growing crimes — it's increased tenfold in the past five years. If you've flipped to this chapter because the information in your social security earnings statement is wrong (and you've already determined you're not dealing with a simple bureaucratic error), you are a victim.

Someone has stolen your social security number and used it to establish a new identity. This person has gotten a new job and his earnings are going on your record. That may be helpful whenever you retire (assuming social security is still solvent by then), but right now, it is undoubtedly doing you a great deal of harm.

Now that they've begun establishing a new identity with your SSN, they've no doubt also obtained credit cards, bank accounts, etc., and are presently in the process of screwing up your credit record.

Put down the book, and get this situation straightened out. The Privacy Rights Clearinghouse (**www.privacyrights.org**) has an excellent fact sheet on-line to help you.

Identity thieves can charge your existing credit card accounts to the limit — and then open up new ones in your name, running up bills you'll be deemed responsible for and ruining your credit record for years to come.

This happened to Jessica Grant, whose good credit was borrowed for three and a half years by a woman out in Wisconsin. By the time she discovered the theft of her identity, there were nineteen accounts in various stages of default — in her name. And the creditors blamed her.

Most damage by identity theft occurs when a person doesn't actively use or obtain credit. The basic correspondence simply doesn't exist. So the thief "borrows" the shell credit data, replaces the address, submits job information, etc., and then starts applying for credit. New credit cards get mailed (to the newly provided address), the bills start coming, and everything is fine, until payments aren't made. An ugly situation for Jessica Grant, that's for sure.

It can get even worse.

The thieves can apply for loans, divert your mail, even transfer property out of your name and into theirs.

You may have read about Irene Silverman, a wealthy Manhattan socialite, missing since the summer of 1998. Two grifters, a mother and her son, targeted Silverman, rented an apartment in her building, and began putting together a scheme to steal her fifteen-million-dollar fortune.

Shortly thereafter, Silverman disappeared.

When the grifters were finally arrested outside the New York Hilton on unrelated charges of a con they'd run in Las Vegas, they had Silverman's birth certificate and her social security card in their possession. The police still strongly suspect they killed her.

Remember, your identity is only as secure as the person who generates your papers chooses it to be. ID can be fraudulently obtained and used by anyone smart enough to hoodwink your local DMV clerk, for example. The process is even easier by mail. The big joke at the New York City Department of Health records department used to be how it was virtually impossible to get anything in person — even with the right paperwork. But all you had to do was send the fifteen-dollar payment by mail and your request would be processed lickety-split. A few well-placed coffee stains on your illegibly filled-out form quickened the process even more.

Any part of your public record is up for grabs to the dedicated con artist or the person who wants to do you harm. The key is to be aware of what's going on. You should check everything you can at least once a year: your credit report, driver's license and motor vehicle information, and real estate-related filings and documentation including mortgages, taxes, and liens. If you periodically check these items, you'll lessen the amount of damages if you are already a victim and, most importantly, you'll be more knowledgeable of the process and better equipped to respond in a timely fashion if you become a victim in the future.

AN OFFER HE COULDN'T REFUSE

When we last left Benny, the bad bald man, I was in the process of confronting him in court with an out-and-out lie he'd told a judge.

The look he gave me during those proceedings would have peeled the paint off a new car.

I soon discovered that Benny had a twenty-year pattern of

destroying anyone who challenged him. He ruined careers, injected and hooked his accusers on drugs, hung their pets, and had their mail forwarded to his address so that he could sort through it at his leisure and do whatever damage he deemed appropriate.

If I wasn't the new man at the top of his hit list, I was close. Definitely in the top ten.

No matter how careful I was, I knew that given enough time, he would find me — and find a way to hurt me. I had to put him off my trail somehow.

As the case continued to unfold, I found myself even more involved with his soon-to-be-ex-in-laws. Benny came to believe (falsely) that I was having an affair with his current wife. He was famous for blaming everyone for everything imaginable under the sun.

I decided to use that to my advantage.

In addition to the money at stake, Benny and his wife were involved in a dispute over custody of their four-year-old son. One particular Thursday, I knew he would be dropping his son off at the exclusive Upper East Side apartment building where his mother — my client — lived.

I brainstormed with the group of associates whose opinions I most trusted. And we went into action.

My associates and I obtained two adjacent parking spaces near the apartment building — not an easy thing to do in Manhattan. I parked my car in one of them. In front of me, we parked a van. Waiting inside the van were two operatives, armed with weapons and a video camera.

After Benny had dropped his son off, I sauntered in carrying a bouquet of flowers.

Benny stood and glared at me as I handed the doorman the flowers. I glared right back at him.

"Could you hold these for me?" I asked the doorman. "I forgot something."

With that, I walked out of the building and back to my car. I pulled a little plastic bag out of the trunk. I walked back in the building, past Benny, picked up my flowers, and took the elevator upstairs . . . not to the wife's apartment, but to the building's athletic club, where I pulled the *New York Post* out of the plastic bag and sat with my flowers, reading, for an hour or so.

As I saw later on videotape, Benny had watched me every step of the way. And when he left the building, he checked out my car. At that point in time, he knew very little about me. If he intended to get back at me, he needed more information.

I wanted to provide him with it.

In the back seat, I had placed a package addressed to Kevin McKeown with the address label clearly visible.

The video showed him walking to my car and studying it for a moment. He didn't look in the back seat. Instead, he walked back towards the building and got into his car, which was double-parked. Then he pulled up alongside my car, got out a pen and paper, and wrote down my license plate number.

He started off down the street — and stopped. He backed up, got out of his car, pen and paper in hand, and double-checked the license plate number. Then he drove away, satisfied he had the information he needed.

He was right.

But he was wrong, too.

Several months later, after I received a death threat, I requested that the authorities revoke Benny's gun permit on the basis that he lied on the gun application.

"How do you know he lied? Gun permit applications are confidential," Sgt. Malone, the head of the gun permit department, asked.

"First, he can't help himself. He's a liar. Second, if he had truthfully answered #4 on your gun application, you wouldn't have given him a permit." Sgt. Malone walked to the other side of the room and pulled Benny's application from a file cabinet. He examined Section #4, which concerned mental disorders and treatment. He smiled.

"He has how many guns?" he asked, shaking his head in amazement. (Remember the arsenal I described in Chapter 5?)

So Benny, not wanting to be outdone, responded with a

complaint accusing me of harassing him. I was able to review details of his complaint at the county clerk's office.

He'd clearly been a busy boy.

The complaint included Kevin McKeown's date of birth, home address, social security number, and more. I suspect he'd hired a private eye and run a credit header (the freely accessed top portion of a credit report), possibly even did a full credit check. I guarantee he went through Kevin McKeown's trash. He had everything he needed to cause a lot of trouble for me — all because I'd given him the chance to write down my license plate number.

Good thing that particular plate actually came back to a different Kevin McKeown. A Kevin McKeown who had nothing in common with me but the name we shared.

Every piece of information he'd obtained about me was wrong.

The false license plate trick has been around for a long time. Back when a great deal of the federal government's attention was focused on organized crime, they used a similar scam. If things were going along a little too smoothly, a government agency — we'll call them the A2Z — would do some active manipulation regarding their target's license plate numbers.

Say one member of a certain family — the Corleones, to borrow a familiar name — drove a 1985 black Cadillac sedan, license plate number ABC-1234. The A2Z boys would get hold of a similar 1985 black Caddy and make up duplicate license plates. These duplicate plates weren't fancy — in fact, they weren't even metal. They were just designed to look like the genuine article from a distance.

Then, A2Z would drive the car with the duplicate plates by another mob family's home or place of business — say, Tagliatelle's restaurant — in the middle of the night. Somebody in the car throws a Molotov cocktail at the front of the restaurant, only reaching as far as the sidewalk where no real damage would be done. There would be a small, harmless sidewalk fire. Of course, A2Z doesn't throw the cocktail without making sure that there are people around. Maybe a guy walking his dog, maybe a few people in a parked car, maybe a couple standing in the shadows of the building: someone to note the license plate.

Then they let nature take its course.

License plate duplication best exemplifies identification manipulation of a nonperson, an object.

This same license plate trick is used in the two parking ticket capitals of the world: New York City and Washington, D.C. Traffic agents pouncing on their prey only write down the plate number, registration dates, make and model, but never make note of that very important Vehicle Identification Number. When was the last time you saw a person writing a parking ticket tap the license plate to see if it's even made out of metal?

I'm not sure if it is still done today, but a while back a New York City taxi fleet owner saved millions with this stunt. Taxicab medallions cost over a quarter-million dollars each. If you ever wondered why New York City looks like a yellow sea of taxis, it just might be because a few dozen yellow clones of one properly registered and authorized taxi are flooding the streets at the same time. Only the drivers look different. Everything else is a copy, a very good copy: license plates, medallion, tag, IDs, registrations, VINs, numbers of every kind. You don't have to be a human computer to figure out that large amounts of money are involved.

PLAY DETECTIVE

Enter the world of secret codes. *Real* secret codes, like the big boys have. You need one now more than ever. There's nothing better to safeguard your identity and your possessions. PIN, security code, access code — whatever you want to call it. You need a good one, one that changes and is easy for only you to remember.

Any good detective, indeed even the clumsiest spy, doesn't settle for a standard, everyday run-of-the-mill security code. Not even if it's changed periodically. Who hasn't forgotten a PIN or security code at some point in his life? (I paced around the base of the Eiffel Tower for two hours once because I couldn't remember a computer access code. Damn French!) Anyway, if you haven't forgotten a code, chances are it's too easy or you've had the same one for too long.

You need a system. Make up your own. One that is very personal to you. It's quite easy. The key is to have a **base number.** This could be anyone's birth date — one you'll always remember. Or the house number of an old friend. Generally, a four to six digit date works well. Then input changing numbers within that number — **a variable number.** I use the number that corresponds with the current month of the year. You could use the number of the current year, plus or minus one.

For example, if your base number is your cat's birthday, July 19, 1996, it would be 71996. If you put the current month number, 4 (for April) in our example here, between the month and the day, your code would become 741996, and next month it would be 751996. The range of possibilities is limitless. Just think of a simple system. One that means something to you, and one that is virtually impossible for a hacker to piece together.

Until you get used to your personal system don't make it too complicated. You'll go crazy. The key is to force yourself into changing the number once a month or every other month (use even- or odd-numbered months).

This is a two-week exercise. During the first week you have to come up with a few base numbers and consider what system of variable numbers would work for you. Then, during the second week, make your decision and mentally test your system's viability. For example, if you haven't thought out what happens when the months go to a double-digit number, you'll be distraught. (Hint: Use the sum of the two digits.)

And how did I remember that computer code in Paris? I walked over to Isle St. Louis and drank some great French wine! It works every time.

PROTECT YOURSELF

1. Once a year check your social security earnings statement. Visit the Social Security Administration Web site at http://www.ssa.gov or call them at 800-772-1213. If you suspect any misuse, call their fraud division at 800-269-0271. Check your statement against your yearly tax earning documentation.

2. Check your credit report at least once a year. See "Protect Yourself" in Chapter 3 for a list of the companies that maintain your credit report and how to reach them.

3. Check the identification constants in your life. If you are concerned about ID theft then at least once a year obtain a summary or statement of your real estate, banking, driver's license, registration, insurance, and credit files. Check for accuracy and possible theft.

4. Maintain a healthy skepticism concerning others' ID. Don't be afraid to ask for it. Politely say, "Before we continue further, please be kind enough to show me some identification." Write down the information and verify it the best you can. Pay close attention to the picture. Once, as a test, I presented the identification of a black female partner as my own and wasn't questioned.

5. When you hire someone — a contractor, a baby-sitter, a helper, a potential employee — check every detail of his or her resume and application. Run a background check. A local investigator can do this for you very inexpensively. Just look in the yellow pages under investigators and shop around. Ask for a sample of their work. Conduct background checks again after a specified period of time. Problems can surface years after you ran an initial check. A person who ran into serious problems after you ran a check may still be watching your child!

12

TOO GOOD TO BE TRUE

THE TROJAN HORSE EFFECT

Pan Am used to be the world's largest airline.

IBM was the biggest name in the computer industry.

And Douglaston Container was one of the country's largest packaging manufacturers, supplying paper containers of all kinds to corporations across the world for close to three decades.

But by 1994, the firm had fallen on hard times — through no fault of its own, as I'd discovered after a week of intensive briefings and investigation.

The fault belonged largely to the balding gentleman lying on the lounge chair across the pool from me. His name was Mark Weyerhaus. He was Douglaston's controller — the guy who was supposed to be watching the company's money.

He'd been watching it go right into his own pocket for the last two years.

I watched him bake in the sun and shook my head. Contentedly sipping his little rum drink, ogling the blond swimming laps (who also happened to be sharing his villa), he obviously considered himself — to quote Lou Gehrig — "the luckiest man on the face of the earth."

I felt like standing up and shouting across to him, "luck had nothing to do with it," but he was going to learn that lesson soon enough.

Weyerhaus wasn't the only one embezzling money from Douglaston. Two other people were involved in the scheme — but he was the brains of the operation that successfully siphoned off millions of dollars from the company through false billings and nonexistent vendors. When Carl Rasoli, a clever ex-federal agent, and I were brought in on the investigation, we immediately zeroed in on him as our target.

But Weyerhaus and his buddies had hidden their tracks well. We knew they'd stolen more than a million dollars, but how much more, we weren't sure. We couldn't pin down the date the embezzlement had started, exactly how many people were involved, who they were, and, most importantly, where the money was. Carl and I had spent a week going through their trash, their credit reports, their public and not-so-public records — and we hadn't found anything.

We decided, therefore, to make something happen, to stir up the pot a little bit, as it were.

It was time Weyerhaus got lucky.

Every Thursday afternoon, Weyerhaus had a habit of going with a small group of cronies to lunch. And when I say habit, I mean a very predictable event. At 1 P.M. sharp, the group of friends, anywhere from four to eight men, would file into their favorite Chinese restaurant, the Golden Temple. We had become very familiar with the Golden Temple since we had tracked this pattern over a five-week period.

On the Thursday afternoon Mark got lucky, we were waiting for him.

Anyone who frequented the shopping plaza in which the Golden Temple restaurant was located became quite accustomed to being asked to buy raffle tickets. So we figured we would join in the fun.

Weyerhaus couldn't resist the attention he received from the young, attractive brunette when he exited the restaurant with his friends. As we'd hoped, Weyerhaus wanted to look generous in front of his friends. He was actually nice enough to pressure his friends into buying tickets from our operative as well. He pulled a crisp new twenty-dollar bill out of his wallet and bought four books of tickets.

One of those turned out to be the winning number.

"I can't believe it," Weyerhaus said the following Monday, when a woman associate I'd hired called to tell him he'd won.

He was still dazed when, later that same day, a messenger showed up with the documents confirming him as the lucky winner.

I suspect that by the time evening rolled around, Weyerhaus was feeling under control enough to call his wife and tell her about the unexpected business conference that had come up at the end of the month. Then he phoned his girlfriend and had her arrange her schedule to share his ten-day, all-expenses-paid trip to the Bahamas.

I wish I could have delivered the tickets to Weyerhaus myself and seen the look on his face, but I had work to do.

Carl and I flew down a week ahead of Weyerhaus to get his villa ready: turn down the sheets, clean the furniture, arrange some fresh flowers, install the bugs in the phone, hide the tiny cameras, wire the whole place for sound, etc.

Then we settled into the villa next to his and waited for the show to begin.

(More about Weyerhaus and the vacation that put him in jail in the following chapter.)

❑ ❑ ❑ ❑ ❑

There are three kinds of luck: good, bad, and what I like to call "creative" — a stroke of good fortune that you make or somebody makes for you.

You've probably been hit with that phone call or postcard

promising you a free vacation . . . the catch turns out to be your required attendance at a presentation selling condominium time-shares. The people running the show hope they'll catch you with your guard down.

Think of it as the "Trojan Horse" effect. Con artists count on your excitement (about a gift of a very large, beautiful horse, for instance) overwhelming your normal sense of caution (concerned that the horse might be filled with enemy warriors). So examine the circumstances surrounding your apparent windfall carefully. Who's giving away the prize? How did you happen to win? Is there any way this prize can be used against you?

The lesson to remember: If something seems too good to be true, it probably is. . . .

MEANER THAN A JUNKYARD DOG

Watching Ben Lota walk down the street was like watching Godzilla rampage through Tokyo.

People moved quickly to get out of his way.

It was partly because Ben was a big guy — about six foot three, 240 pounds, solid muscle all the way through.

It was also because Ben looked like the thug that he was — like if he needed to hurt you to get something, he wouldn't think twice about it.

Ben did his hurting — and his threatening, stealing, and other petty crimes — on behalf of his boss, a con artist who'd parlayed a lifetime's worth of scams into a nice estate on Long Island and a veneer of social respectability.

I'd been hired to rip that veneer off and put Ben's boss (whose name I can't reveal because of ongoing litigation) behind bars where he belonged.

The first thing we decided to do was get a complete picture of the scope of Ben's, and thus the boss's, activities.

So we called Ben up at home and made him an offer he couldn't refuse:

"Yeah?"

"Hello, can I speak to Ben Lota?"

"This is Lota. What do you want?"

"Ben, my name is Jamie Johnson, and I'm calling from Dunwoody Cellular. We'd like to offer you a free cellular phone and two free months of cellular phone service."

"Yeah, well, I don't need a cellular phone."

"Well, Ben, a lot of people feel that way, but this is a free offer. You can use the phone for two months at no charge whatsoever, then decide if you want to keep it or not."

"What's the catch?"

"There is no catch, Ben. No hidden charges either — we promise. It's part of a marketing test promotion. If you agree, the phone will be Express-Mailed to you for delivery tomorrow. The one thing we do ask is at the end of the two months you fill out a survey for us."

"Huh." Ben was silent a moment. "No charges, huh?"

I smiled. "No charges," I said. "And you'll see that in writing."

A female "postal worker" delivered the phone to Ben the next day.

True to our word, we never charged Ben a dime for the service.

The phone wasn't free, of course. It was simply one that we'd requested under an assumed name and address. But we happily paid Ben's bills.

After all, we then owned a list of two months' worth of his outgoing — and incoming — phone calls. Which gave us some very solid information to start our investigation with.

❏ ❏ ❏ ❏ ❏

Free is a very powerful word. It can turn a group of well-mannered shoppers into a horde of stampeding animals. It can cause the most careful businessman in the world to override his lifelong training. Free appeals to a very basic human instinct: greed. There are other very basic instincts as well, of course. . . .

INSTINCT APPEAL:
HOOK, LINE, AND SINKER

Every good pretext will appeal to a wide array of human needs, desires, or emotions.

It's like marketing and advertising.

And just like in advertising, sex works. . . .

Willem Barnelhoff lived on the intercoastal waterway in Boca Raton, Florida. There was always some sort of construction going on around his home. A new wing here, a new pool bathhouse there. Willem's partners in his investment banking firm wanted to know what he did in his spare time besides serving as construction manager to the latest building project. He had told them that because of a painful back problem, he would be working from home through the summer. The partners believed Willem was violating their confidentiality agreement by secretly acting in concert with a competing firm with a sleazy reputation. They feared massive SEC problems that would end up costing them millions.

They wanted Willem followed. We couldn't even establish what he looked like. He had a foreign driver's license and a house staff that buffered any attempt at a direct approach. He had always been suspicious about being followed so we didn't want to risk that. Every automobile that exited through the locked metal gates had heavily tinted windows.

Enter beautiful Cathy. By boat. In her bikini.

It took two days to make sure she wouldn't destroy the small motorboat I had rented. And hours to show her how to use the boat anchor and to quickly determine which end of a fishing rod was to be held in her hand.

I got worried when she told me that she didn't even enjoy eating fish and the thought of catching one fully grossed her out.

Willem's construction workers couldn't help themselves: No work was getting done. A full day of barely audible pleas from the boys with the hammers on shore left me optimistic a mile away listening by radio and trying to catch up on some sleep in a car.

Cathy flashed an occasional smile and enthusiastic wave but pretended to be fully preoccupied with her book and fishing pole. She would disappear into the small cabin to radio me and to further the imagination of the shore-bound studs.

"I'm petrified. What the hell am I going to do if a fish bites my line?"

"Don't worry. One of your boyfriends there will probably dive in to help."

It took another two days before our construction workers came up with a plan. One of the hammering hunks must have begged a buddy to casually cruise by in his boat around lunchtime. "Let's go for a quick spin," the boater suggests to his friend. Then, "Oh, pretty girl, you're still here. I barely noticed. Catch anything?"

He was about to get caught — hook, line, and sinker — by Cathy.

Before long her boat was docked next to Willem's boat. She lounged at the pool while her new friend, Tyler, went about his work. It didn't take long for her to get inside to use the bathroom and telephone. A quick look at family photos found Cathy confident she'd be able to ID Willem. And she did, the next day, at the offices of the competing investment banking firm.

FOR ME?

"I just love flowers," she said. "Who are they from?"

I wasn't too happy about handing over that beautiful vase packed with exotic flowers. The damn thing had cost me $120. She placed the vase on a small table just inside the front door and buried her nose in a bloom.

"There's a card," I said. I presented my clipboard that had, of course, a little form. A receipt of delivery form. I'd made it myself just that morning at Kinko's.

"Sign at the X. Please print your name and phone number below."

She spoke her name out loud as she wrote: "Elena D'Angeles."

"Thank you," I said.

I didn't get a tip. But I was content. I would soon find out all about her. And by knowing who she was, we would gain access to the person we were really after: Jeff Hutchinson, the con man we'd been monitoring for months both in the states and in the U.K. He had defrauded dozens of upstanding businessmen. A few had sought our aid in bringing his antics to an end. Jeff and his boyfriend had a habit of renting out rooms to single females. Once Jeff had settled into his new apartment we knew it was only a matter of time before a classified ad would appear in a local paper. And we needed to learn whether the new subtenant, Elena in this case, could be recruited to help us either directly or indirectly to get to Jeff.

By the way, the card simply said "A secret admirer. I'll see you soon, my love."

Gifts break down many barriers and come in all sizes, shapes, and packages. . . .

PARTY FAVORS

"I got a little present here for you," Captain Tinslet said.

"Excellent," I said. "Can we keep doing it once or twice a week until further notice?"

"I see no reason why not."

There's only one statement uttered more frequently by law enforcement officers than "I want a doughnut." Although it sounds a little like a question, it's a statement. A powerful statement.

"Do me a favor."

These four words usually proceed a request that law enforcement brothers and sisters are almost always too happy to comply with.

The telephone call spanned two time zones, twenty-one

hundred miles, a dozen states, and three minutes of my time. The police captain near Flagstaff, Arizona, was happy to help.

He had originally told me when we spoke that if he didn't collect our suspect's trash himself, he'd have one of his guys do it or he'd simply get the local garbage company to pick it up.

Before the garbage truck headed for the dump that morning it stopped off at the police station to hand-deliver the catch of the day. From the men in the garbage truck to the men in blue.

"Can you overnight it to me? It's important stuff," I asked.

"Sure, no problem. Oh, should I send it the way it is or gift-wrap it?" Funny. I laughed, of course. I wanted those gifts to keep on coming.

PLAY DETECTIVE

You and a partner are both to list five items both of you gave to people in the last year. Then make a list of five items you've received.

In your mind, trace the source of those gifts. Where did they come from? Where did the person get the gift before they gave it to you?

Now, perform the same exercise on the five most recent people to have entered your life. Trace their origins in your mind. Do you really know?

PROTECT YOURSELF

1. Have a healthy skepticism when you win a prize. Ask questions. Officials of legitimate contests will have all the right answers and be able to confirm everything in writing. Never participate in a "contest" that requires any type of fee. They are either scams or a vehicle used to get you on their profitable mailing list.

2. Be skeptical about unexpected gifts. Believe it or not, some wackos have been known to deliver gift items with listening and video surveillance devices in them. If you have concerns just be careful and physically check the item, especially if it's electric: a TV, clock, air conditioner (believe it or not), radio, answering machine, telephone, VCR, computer, coffee maker.

3. Watch for the reverse gift. A reverse gift comes out of nowhere. If I'm investigating you and discover you have a car for sale, you bet I'll want to test-drive it. Then I'll have to use your bathroom. I'll scan the house and create a reverse gift: "I see you have an old TV. I sell TVs. I can get it for you at cost." Or "Is that computer for sale? It's exactly what my daughter wants." I'll try to make you an offer you just won't be able to refuse.

Once when scanning the classifieds, we discovered that our target had a computer for sale. You bet we purchased that computer and found, much to our delight, that we were able to recover essential evidence off the hard drive.

4. Watch your signature. It could be a free gift from you to a nosy person or a forger. Have bad handwriting or print your name where you are to sign.

13

TOURIST TRAPS

ON THE BEACH

Back to the "luckiest man on earth" — Mark Weyerhaus.

We'd arranged for Weyerhaus and his lady friend to stay in one of the most beautiful, relaxing spots in the Bahamas. A small, secluded development, located on a tiny spit of land, with the ocean on one side and an inlet sheltering local fishing boats on the other. They were in a modern, fully furnished, beautifully decorated villa with all the amenities: big-screen cable television, completely stocked kitchen, screened-in porch overlooking the ocean, and cameras and microphones hidden in virtually every room.

All that equipment was wired back (through an adjoining wall) into the villa next door, where Carl and I were parked in similar style. We could watch Weyerhaus's every move on our big-screen TV. If things got slow, we could always change over to the Giants game or HBO — we had VCRs getting every moment in every room down on tape.

The problem was, nothing much was happening.

We got a little more invasive. While Weyerhaus and the blond were off taking a boat trip one day, Carl went in their room (of course we had the keys — we had paid for the place!) and copied the contents of both his computer and date book . . .

Which still didn't lead us anywhere.

We had wanted Weyerhaus to relax and let down his guard a little. Now it seemed we'd done our job too well. Weyerhaus was having such a good time, he wasn't talking to anyone about anything. Aside from a call or two to his wife to tell her what a lousy time he was having at the conference and how he really missed her and their son, he didn't say a word about his life back in the States. I'd lay odds that Douglaston Container never crossed his mind at all.

So Carl and I decided to launch a torpedo.

We placed a phone call back to the States, to a couple of our friends. Richie and Frank were both ex-cops who not only looked the part, but also had the demeanor of Roman Catholic priests. One look at these two guys and you would know a) they were cops, and b) you could believe every word they said.

We told them to stop by Weyerhaus's home and office the next day and ask to speak to him on a personal matter. When told he wasn't there, they were to ask his wife and his number-two man at Douglaston, Scott Goldman (who was also in on the embezzling scam), pointed questions about Weyerhaus. Questions that would make Weyerhaus and his cronies think the law was coming after them.

Carl and I kicked back with some conch fritters and rum, ran a couple of tests on the equipment, and waited for the calls to roll in.

We'd told Richie and Frank to make their rounds as early as possible — we knew that Weyerhaus would stay out late and try to sleep in. The earlier any calls for him came, the more likely he'd be groggy and spill the beans.

The first call came from Goldman at 9:15 A.M.

"Hello?"

"Mark? It's Scott."

"Scott?" You could hear the gears grinding painfully in

Weyerhaus's head — did he know a Scott? "What time is it?"

"It's nine-fifteen. Listen, some cops or IRS agents or something were just here, and. . . ."

"Wait." He cut Goldman off. "Where are you calling from?"

"A pay phone. It's safe."

I had to give Weyerhaus credit. He'd woken up pretty quick. But he should have been just as worried about the security of his own phone line.

Goldman told Weyerhaus about the two men who'd stopped by. Clearly the law. Weyerhaus wanted to know what they were after.

"They didn't say," Goldman replied. "Your wife said they stopped at your house, too. I told her I was going to call you."

"At the sales conference, right?"

"Don't worry — it's covered."

They kept talking. Was the law really onto them? Should Weyerhaus stay out of the country? Should Goldman come join him? Should they rendezvous at the Phoenix property?

Phoenix property?

Carl and I looked at each other.

Bingo.

A public records search of all real estate purchased in Phoenix during the previous year revealed that only about 10 percent of all property transfers were done under a corporate name. We had every one of those transfers checked. After numerous days of searching and reviewing every piece of paper, we found the right one — the one that led us to Weyerhaus's mail drop, his bank account, and what remained of the embezzled money.

Weyerhaus and his cohorts were later arrested for fraud and conspiracy. During the trial, his lawyer tried to have the evidence we'd obtained in the Bahamas thrown out of court.

"It's illegal," he cried. "It was illegally obtained."

The judge reminded him that although it might be illegal to tap phone lines in the United States, the activity took place outside the United States — and outside of his jurisdiction.

Which was one of the reasons we'd shipped Weyerhaus to the Bahamas in the first place.

❑ ❑ ❑ ❑ ❑

Whole industries (in fact, entire countries) depend on the generosity — and frequent lapses in taste — of the American tourist.

Consider those awful double-decker tour buses parked next to the Empire State Building. No self-respecting New Yorker would be caught dead riding one of them. He'd rather lick a subway platform with his tongue. And no city dweller would pay more than $1.25 for a big pretzel. Tourists from Des Moines gladly fork over two bucks.

Meanwhile, when a New Yorker visits Iowa, he or she will shell out twenty bucks for a *Field of Dreams* T-shirt that Des Moines residents wouldn't pay more than fifty cents for.

Lapses in judgment like those are okay — after all, you go on vacation to relax and have a good time. You want to step away from your workday cares and worries and leave all your troubles at home.

Just don't leave your common sense there, too.

Call this one the "Disneyland Effect." Budgets go out the window, ugly souvenirs get bought, guards go down, total strangers become best friends and are invited into your hotel room . . .

Where they proceed to rob you blind.

Con artists, swindlers, and all types of dangerous crooks congregate around wealthy tourists with money to spend. Don't be a victim. Follow the same common-sense rules on the road that you would at home.

NOW BOARDING:
WANDERING EYES

It was shortly before eight o'clock in the morning. The instructions seemed simple. To the person giving them to me, anyway.

"Drop everything and focus on Jack Naiman. Find out where he's going and go with him."

"Do we have any idea where he might be going?" I asked.

"Somewhere out of the country, I'd guess. Every source says the same thing: He's real secret about where he's going and hasn't told anyone anything. He's probably leaving tonight or tomorrow."

Naiman's company had, for well over a ten-year period, enjoyed the exclusive right in the United States to sell construction boots with the Caterpillar name attached. Caterpillar was entitled to a percentage-of-sales licensing fee and, of course, normal auditing access to the financial books.

It turned out that Naiman was glad to produce Caterpillar documents showing how many pairs of boots were coming from his Chinese manufacturer. He just forgot to reveal that he had more than one manufacturer. So for every one pair of boots Caterpillar was making a small licensing fee on, three or four other pairs were flooding the U.S. market without the fee being paid.

Oh, and Naiman also forgot to pay Uncle Sam his percentage of the tens of millions of dollars he was making.

Jack Naiman lived on Long Beach Island, a thirty-minute ride to JFK airport, the gateway to the world. Dozens of airlines would be sending planes to hundreds of destinations within the next thirty-six hours.

It took me one hour to find Naiman's Northwest Airlines reservation to Tokyo. He was scheduled to take off in less than five hours on the 1:50 P.M. flight from JFK.

As I headed to the airport, arrangements were to be made to place me in the seat next to Naiman. But a problem developed. He was one of a party of two, and since the business class section only sat two across, I would have to be content with sitting directly behind him. Unfortunately, I would not be the hoped-for "traveling eyes" on the flight.

During a flight, as a target reviews paperwork concerning an anticipated meeting, the investigator on the target's tail reviews it, too. The traveling eyes are usually sitting right next to the target or at an angle in the row behind him.

But Jack was traveling with an unidentified male, so I'm even more frustrated. A few quick peeks in his briefcase while he visits the bathroom are out of the question.

I look about as Asian as an American flag, so after we arrived in Tokyo, my job consisted of simply following the operatives following Naiman along the journey through Taipei, Taichung, Hong Kong, and mainland China.

My clean-up role involved using my American appearance in the only way I could. As a precaution, in case the half-dozen people following Naiman lost him (which is easy to do), I would approach the hotel checkout counter ten minutes after Naiman had driven away from the hotel.

"Yeah, hi. My dad just checked out. Naiman's the name. You forgot to give him a copy of his bill. You know, the hotel receipt."

Apologies would accompany the quick production of the hotel bill, which would include telephone numbers of places where he would probably be showing up in the not-too-distant future.

We were able to piece together where and how the fraud and tax evasion stunts were pulled off, including the amounts down to the dollar.

Naiman, and, as it turned out, his son-in-law traveling companion, might not have been too happy upon their arrival back into the United States, but Uncle Sam and Caterpillar Enterprises were certainly grinning ear to ear. U.S. Customs and IRS criminal agents escorted Naiman to a secure environment upon his arrival back at JFK.

A very simple concept many business travelers ignore: Eyes see.

The chances are very good that there is at least one set of traveling eyes on any given international flight departing from the United States.

Being on the road makes business executives an inviting target for all different kinds of con artists. If you travel frequently as part of your job, it pays for you to not only pay attention to your surroundings, but to think about what your patterns of behavior reveal to anyone who might be watching you. Take a moment and go back to the first chapter of this book. Flip through it.

Then read on.

WHO'S WATCHING WHOM

Everyone liked Rob Beveridge. He was an intelligent, honest, upright lawyer for Worthington Securities, a popular Wall Street investment firm. A good friend, a great husband, and a loving father who, according to papers recently filed by the SEC, was guilty of insider trading.

"No way. Never," Rich Deitz said as he glared at each one of us. Deitz was lead counsel for Worthington Securities. Right now, he was looking at my two partners and me as if we were the Three Stooges.

Rob Beveridge had been Worthington's most successful dealmaker for six years in a row. But some strange things had begun happening recently involving every deal he worked on. The SEC called it insider trading. Deitz called it baloney.

I was impressed with Deitz. I thought his reputation was accurate: an aggressive, knowledgeable, honest attorney. One of my partners on the case, Aaron Jamieson, disagreed.

"Deitz is lying. He's probably involved in the scam," Aaron said as we left the meeting.

Now Aaron was no dope. A lot of people liked Aaron. The U.S. government liked Aaron. They liked him so much they put him through law school. He fumed at the notion of any attorney who might give the legal profession a bad name with sleazy antics.

For nearly three months we monitored Beveridge: joining him at movies, visiting his relatives in Toronto, cheering his kid's soccer teams. We analyzed every charge he made on his credit cards. We thoroughly researched his phone calls. We even traveled with him for the four or five days a month he traveled. Nothing. If this guy was involved in insider trading he was covering his tracks pretty well.

On our second road trip with Rob, we ended up at the Marriott Crystal City in Arlington, Virginia, just a stone's throw across the Potomac from Washington, D.C. Rob was an easy guy to follow, not suspicious and a safe driver. He'd made three stops on the trip down from New York: lunch with a relative in Wilmington, Delaware; a planned twenty-minute meeting outside Baltimore with clients; and a two-hour dinner with his son, a plebe at the Naval Academy in Annapolis, Maryland.

We didn't take any chances, though. We'd had a satellite transmitter attached to the underside of his silver Lexus.

Rob checked into the Marriott a little after 8 P.M. We checked into the room directly across the hall on the eighth floor.

Aaron, who had run to a 7-Eleven for snacks, entered the room a short while later.

Aaron was excited. And Aaron never got excited.

"I just rode up the elevator with a guy I recognized from the Albany Hilton that Rob visited three weeks ago."

"A lot of people who hang around New York's capital have been known to frequent the D.C. area," I suggested.

"I don't like it. Something's wrong," Aaron said.

Later that evening we were joined by two associates from D.C. We decided to run the license plates of every car parked in the hotel's garage. We started with the seventeen New York and New Jersey plates. By 3 A.M., database searches had revealed that an automobile registered to a retired New York City policeman, now a New York State-licensed private investigator, was parked in the Marriott parking garage.

Before noon we had this P.I.'s hotel records, his home and business telephone records, and, most telling, his cell-phone bills.

Aaron was wrong. Deitz was right when he said Rob wouldn't get involved in insider trading. At least knowingly.

Subsequent investigation revealed that a rival Wall Street brokerage firm had been following Rob (and pulling his phone records) for nearly two years. They simply reviewed whom Rob was communicating and meeting with and then monitored, and more often than not invested in, companies Rob had been interacting with.

Rob had no reason to think he was being followed. In fact, he would later laugh incredulously and say, "I lead such a simple, normal life. Who in their right mind would want to follow me?"

That's exactly the right question to ask. Who would want to follow you on a business trip? Who would gain by knowing something about you?

Take out a pen and paper, and conduct the following exercise.

PLAY DETECTIVE

First, think of the competition. Whether you're a monk, a salesperson, a politician, a broker of any kind, a team coach, a business owner, or an academic, you've got someone who would be quite happy to have your position, your clients, or simply a percentage of your profits.

Think about how you might unintentionally be revealing useful information to your competitors.

You don't have to be a Rhodes Scholar to figure out why Donald Trump is walking around some empty lot in midtown Manhattan at midnight. Just hurry up and go buy that small building across the street. Its value is about to go up!

PROTECT YOURSELF

1. **Assume you're a target when traveling.** You're a fish out of water, easily distracted, and more receptive to new and unusual occurrences. Be aware of your surroundings and your vulnerability.

2. **Watch what you review and work on while you're in flight or in an airport boarding area.** If you are very, very concerned, have a traveling companion watch for traveling eyes.

3. **Be more discreet regarding your travel plans.** Communicate your concern to all those who might unknowingly provide bad-intentioned strangers with details of your trip.

Thieves want to know when you're on vacation and a competitor just might want to know what company you are visiting for an important meeting.

4. Learn the local laws at your vacation and business destinations. For instance, wiretapping is illegal in the U.S., but no big deal in England. Trash-picking is a favorite law enforcement pastime in the U.S. Try it in the U.K. and you'll wind up in front of a firing squad.

5. Demand that travel-related companies respect your privacy. Con men and investigators pretext, on a regular basis, all travel-related companies to develop leads and gather information. If you have special concerns, advise hotels, tour operators, airlines, and car rental companies that information should not be discussed without a security code and a confirmation number.

6. Don't advertise information about yourself while traveling. Don't review travel and personal documents in public. Remove the standard name/address tags from your luggage. They're too easy to read. Replace them with tags that have flaps that have to be unclipped or unzipped.

14

SURVEILLANCE TOYS

THE BLACK BOX

Two men were guarding the door.

Another two were acting as lookouts down on the street.

From the day I had arrived in London, I'd been followed. My phone had been tapped, my hotel room bugged, my luggage searched. All to make sure that I had no connection to the authorities — that I was, in fact, who I seemed.

That I posed no threat to the man sitting across the desk from me, an unassuming, fiftyish gentleman who, appearances to the contrary, was a highly wanted person, the prime target of an international sting operation the U.S. government had spent a great deal of time and money setting up.

The man's name was Anthony Kerry.

His crime was engineering, constructing, and selling the world's most sought-after piece of surveillance equipment. Street name: the black box.

"I'd like to buy three dozen," I said. "Possibly more."

Kerry steepled his fingertips, elbows on desk, and frowned.

"It will take us at least a month to construct that many," he said, leaning back in his chair.

Kerry's office was located in an apartment above his store — an operation that sold surveillance equipment to the trade. You only saw Kerry if you were very serious about the information-gathering business, if you had scheduled an appointment — and if Kerry could determine beforehand that you had the money to do business with him.

And you only got a black box if Kerry trusted you.

These state-of-the-art devices were assembled in the U.K. from specifically engineered components constructed around the world, in locations as far-flung as mainland China and Japan.

Roughly the size of a phone book, Kerry's black box was an incredibly versatile piece of gear. From any telephone in the world, you could listen through the sensitive built-in mike, using it as a room monitor. You could download what the device had overheard via modem to your computer. The boxes were designed to be used in series, so that if you had more than one installed at a location, you could switch between them and actually follow someone as they walked from one room to the next.

You could expect to pay on the order of six thousand dollars for a single black box.

In the U.K., they were perfectly legal, legitimate tools of the surveillance trade. They were outlawed in the United States.

Kerry would only deliver these devices to his American customers through the U.S. mail, and because postal inspectors were on the alert for them, only one out of four ever got through to its intended recipient.

Nonetheless, the demand for the black box, largely from drug dealers, other organized-crime figures, and very nosey businessmen, was so high that you could expect to wait anywhere from one to six months for delivery.

I'd called Kerry on my arrival in England and told him I represented the interests of a large investment-banking firm whose name I could not mention. I also told him we were interested in purchasing a number of his devices.

Finally, after a series of phone calls, my request for a meeting was granted. I'm sure Kerry wanted the time to check me out, which we'd anticipated. We had leased phone lines for our "company" and hired a woman to pose as our switchboard operator. I conducted several conversations with my colleagues in the "home office" regarding our business and our hope that we'd be able to purchase the black boxes from Kerry. And just so Kerry would think that we could be connected to a larger, more well-known firm, we placed numerous telephone calls to a firm where an operative had gotten a low-level position with a very important voicemail box on the company telephone network. If our plant was out sweeping floors or picking up mail, we'd simply leave an important "confidential" voicemail message indicating that everything was going well. We knew Kerry would be listening.

My real goal, though, was not to buy the devices, but to lure Kerry to the United States, so he could be arrested.

I almost had him. I agreed to put a hundred thousand cash down on a big order. As part of the deal, Kerry and a few of his technicians were to fly into New York and oversee the devices' installation and the necessary training.

We shook hands on the terms.

We made plane reservations.

I checked out of my hotel and went to the airport.

But Kerry never showed — at the last possible minute, he backed out.

A few months later, the FBI closed the net on its sting operation, formally declaring war on surveillance devices like the black box.

Needless to say, I doubt Kerry will be flying over to this side of the pond (as the British like to call the Atlantic) anytime soon.

❏ ❏ ❏ ❏ ❏

On April 6, 1995, the FBI sting that had targeted Kerry made the front page of the *New York Times,* under the headline "U.S. Agents Raid Stores in 24 Cities to Seize Spy Gear."

During the government's seventeen-month investigation, they tracked shipments of over four thousand illegal devices, including a few dozen black boxes, with a street price of close to $3 million. More than a dozen people were arrested as a result of the operation, for violating the 1968 Omnibus Crime and Safe Streets Act, which makes it illegal for ordinary citizens to own high-tech eavesdropping equipment for "the surreptitious interception of wire, oral, or electronic communications."

Those numbers only hint at the size of the ever-growing market for high-tech surveillance toys.

Toys like Kerry's black box — which enable dirt-diggers everywhere to engage in the kind of wholesale information-gathering we've been talking about throughout this book.

Mirrors that hide television cameras. Briefcases fitted with microphones. Voice stress analyzers. Bulletproof vests.

These toys aren't just being sold to crooks.

They're being bought by working parents who want to see how their nannies really treat the kids. By suspicious husbands who want to keep an eye on their wives. By business executives who want to monitor their employees.

And, of course, by all levels of the government.

Realize that at any moment, you might be under surveillance. Think back over the last six months. I'm sure you can quickly bring to mind five occasions when you would have been horrified to find that a tape recorder had been recording you without your knowledge.

If you saw the movie *Enemy of the State*, you know that this isn't just idle speculation. You have an idea of the kinds of things this technology is capable of.

If you haven't seen the movie, just think about how many times you were filmed by a video camera today. At the ATM, the gas station, the clothing store, your apartment complex.

Soon, there really will be no place to hide.

And don't think just hopping in your car and driving off will make the situation any better. . . .

TRACKING DEVICES

Large trucking companies now routinely install tracking devices on all truck trailers and truck cabs. These devices can map, in real-time, the vehicle's exact location, down to a street address. Fleet owners can monitor shipments from pick-up to drop-off, ensuring their customers accurate delivery information. The owners can make sure their drivers don't squeeze in too many hours behind the wheel. They also act as extra insurance against truck highjacking teams.

These trackers are coming to a car near you very soon.

Financial institutions and insurance companies will require that all vehicles possess tracking devices to safeguard against theft and nonpayment of auto loans. The device will be similar to the LoJack system, virtually impossible to remove or disable. Anytime your vehicle's whereabouts need to be ascertained, the transmitting device will be activated, and its exact location — down to the street address — will be revealed.

Other uses for this device will surely follow.

Here's one that's taking shape already, thanks to companies like Davis Instruments in California. Their DriveRight Monitor goes on your car's sun visor or on the dash. It records information such as the maximum speed the car reaches, how far the car travels, and how long it was driven.

Parents are using it to monitor their kid's driving habits.

There's nothing wrong, per se, with making sure your teen is following safe driving rules, but certain kinds of con artists live to find ways to abuse this kind of new technology.

❏ ❏ ❏ ❏ ❏

The technology used against you is, most often, very subtle. And very simple. Don't expect to see Sean Connery wandering into your office, dressed as a plumber, with tiny wires sticking out of his back pocket. In the real world, anything goes. . . .

DON'T SAY ANYTHING,
I'LL BE RIGHT BACK

My partner, Russel, and I really did have to go to the bathroom. Even if we had previously planned our departure from the table.

"I don't like having my time wasted like this," Russel snapped as he threw his napkin down on his plate of ketchup-covered French fries and headed to the men's room.

I was right behind him, "Oh, would you calm down?"

We left our two dining guests alone at the table to think about our most recent heated round of conversation. The Spellman brothers — Mikey and Johnny — weren't easy to pressure but we made it perfectly clear that we wouldn't be doing any more business with them unless they could deliver — like they had promised.

Stolen airline ticket stock is a large multimillion-dollar fraud problem. If blank tickets get into the wrong hands, like the Spellman brothers', the documents are like blank checks. Run those tickets through a computer printer and you're off. Anywhere you want to go. We had already purchased, at two different times, a total of two hundred blank tickets for forty thousand cash.

But Mikey and Johnny, if those were, in fact, their real names, were very careful, cautious fellows. Before they could be arrested it was important to find out if they were the brains behind the operation or just fronting for someone.

Russel would always order a platter of some kind for "the wife" at home near the end of our little meetings with the Spellman brothers. They'd get restless and always leave the diner before us. Which was fine with us because we always had to recover the tape recorder we had taped under the table. It was always easy to get on but the cement-like tape we used made it very difficult and very noisy to remove.

Four months after we started buying the stolen tickets we got our first break.

At the end of a conversation during one of our creatively planned absences from the table, Johnny had exploded at Mikey:

"You idiot. You ever show up at Express again, I'll smack you. Stay away from there."

"It'll never happen again," Mikey promised.

"And you ever call me Vinny Moscuti again, I'll kill you!"

It took us a few days to figure out the Express was a delivery service that good ole Vinny owned. His delivery people scoped out travel agencies that could that be hit a few weeks later for their stock of tickets.

PLAY DETECTIVE

Sorry to keep making you the target, but you are one. You just might not fully realize it.

Develop a list of places a competitor, enemy, or information thief could hide a voice-activated microcassette recorder in your office: behind a file cabinet, taped under the desk, squeezed under all the computer wires, etc. Then develop a time frame within which someone could plant and recover the recorder for easy listening later that night. Perhaps twenty minutes before your usual morning arrival or as you predictably dash out the door at closing time.

What incriminating information could be gleaned from those recordings?

PROTECT YOURSELF

1. **Watch what you say.** Assume your conversations are being recorded. Especially in emergency-type situations, such as domestic violence. Surveillance toys are getting cheaper and smaller and harder to detect all the time.

2. **Don't just look for sophisticated equipment.** I can leave a simple tape recorder in my jacket while I leave the meeting to go to the bathroom. Or place a voice-activated microcassette

recorder inside an air vent or behind books on a bookshelf. How are you going to protect against that?

3. **Don't assume you can spot the evidence of technological trickery.** I once placed a pin-hole camera through the back of my jacket pointing at a subject while holding a recorder/monitor in my hands. The subject, of course, thought he was looking at the back of my head and felt unthreatened and unobserved. I peacefully watched the entire conversation and transaction he carried out. Another time, we lowered a camera lens fifty feet from the top of an office building so we could look inside a subject's window.

THE LIMITATIONS OF TECHNOLOGY

AN INSIDE JOB

You could see it was tearing the guy apart.

Dominic Capelli was seventy-five years old. He'd spent his whole life building up the New Jersey manufacturing company that bore his name. He'd started off in 1956 making automotive tools and diversified from there. Everything he tried made money; every idea he had turned out to be right.

Dominic ran the creative end of the business — he was never very good with the day-to-day stuff. But he hired the best people and paid them handsomely to supervise his operation. He had a generous profit-sharing plan. He provided good health insurance.

Now it looked like the people he'd trusted to run his company were robbing him blind.

In 1993, when he'd turned seventy, Dominic had stepped away from Capelli Manufacturing. He'd stayed on the board of directors and was still the company's largest shareholder — but he'd turned the reins over. Dominic spent his time enjoying his family, traveling, and staying active — playing tennis, jogging, skiing, etc. That is, until he'd badly sprained his ankle over the summer. He'd had to sit still for weeks.

It was right then, as he described it to me, that he began to get a gut feeling that something was very wrong at his company.

He didn't have anything concrete to go on but he wanted both the CFO and president of his company checked out.

I made a full inquiry over a two-week period and found nothing alarming, nothing unusual. The CFO's and president's apparent incomes and their lifestyles seemed reasonable.

Dominic still felt uneasy. He wanted to see how the company was working, from the inside out.

He tried to get a little more involved at the office himself. He figured that everyone would write off his presence as temporary and be content to give him the run of the place while his ankle healed. But he made everyone uncomfortable — no one was happy to see him back at work. Which only deepened his suspicions and brought us to where we were today . . .

Sitting outdoors on his screened-in porch, sipping coffee, with him authorizing me to break into his own company.

"It's not gonna be easy," he said.

Then he told me about the alarm system they'd had installed throughout the manufacturing complex (which was the size of five football fields) and the adjoining administrative offices.

"It cost a quarter-million dollars," he said. There were passcodes to enable you to access the building after hours, but Dominic had been so far up the corporate ladder (and disconnected from the company's everyday operations when the system was installed) that he'd never had one. And he couldn't ask for one now without raising suspicions.

I was going to have to figure out a way past the alarm system all on my own.

I started the very next day by walking into the complex's main building and asking directions to the employment offices. I was here, I told them, to apply for a job. This gave me somewhat of a license to roam. I found the cafeteria, an employee lounge, the executive offices, and (finally) the men's room, which I sorely needed at that point in my travels.

As I stood at the urinal, trying to plan my next step, I happened to glance up at the window above me.

There was Capelli's quarter-million-dollar alarm system.

I was not impressed.

There were metal strips running all around the glass, making an electrical connection. If that connection was broken, an alarm would sound and the guards (and eventually, the cops) would show up.

Since it was the middle of the workday, I figured that this particular trigger point would not be activated, as most systems are either completely on or completely turned off. So I reached up, disconnected the wires, and pulled them away from the window.

Then I reconnected them, laying them down in front of the glass.

Now the window was no longer part of the security system. I unlatched the window lock.

Later that evening, a little before midnight, I pulled open the window from the other side — and led a team of three men into the company's executive suites.

We searched everything in the president's and CFO's offices. I had a computer expert to crack their security codes, a lockpicker to get into their file cabinets, and a surveillance expert to bug their phones. Boxes of copied files were passed out the small bathroom window. We worked from midnight until 5 A.M. for five nights straight.

We found evidence confirming Dominic's worst fears.

The CFO and president had created an entirely new company on paper — a company that on the surface appeared to be in direct competition with Capelli. Except this company was supplied with product from Dominic's concern to sell without the associated labor and raw material costs.

Dominic at least had the opportunity to have a little revenge. After we had the goods on the CFO and president, he went into the CFO's office and started asking very specific questions. The man turned a pale shade of green when he realized the game was up.

Both men were, of course, fired. They quickly agreed to repay all misappropriated funds to avoid criminal prosecution.

A few days later, I visited Dominic at the manufacturing plant. After catching up, I asked him to join me in the men's room. I received a weird look, until I showed him the window, the wire, and the way I'd gotten into his plant.

He dumped the alarm system, installed extensive video-recording equipment, and hired a team of security guards.

Dominic now pays for an outside forensic accounting firm to review his operation each quarter.

❑ ❑ ❑ ❑ ❑

Dominic's ex-employees spent a quarter-million dollars on an alarm system, trusting it would protect not just the company, but the dirty secrets they were hiding as well.

Talk about misplaced faith. . . .

Don't make the same mistake. While some security technologies are advancing by leaps and bounds, the basic concept behind the alarm system hasn't changed in years: Something happens and a loud noise goes off.

Here's the modern version: Something happens and the system telephones a central monitoring station and/or the police.

Problem number one: No one pays attention to alarms anymore. They're just nuisances (thank car alarms for putting the nail in that coffin).

Problem number two: If the telephone wire is cut, the system can't call anyone (less than 2 percent of the alarm systems today are equipped with a feature that checks your phone line on an ongoing basis).

Motion detectors? Most of them are at the typical points of entry — front and rear doors. Once you're inside, you can disable them.

Even if an alarm does go off, if the cops come and don't see any signs of forced entry, odds are they're going to think it was a false alert.

I have personal knowledge of many a robbery that has taken

place with cops outside the building, securing the entrance.

Think about it. An old-fashioned alarm actually helps the thief more than the property owner. It tells him to get the hell out quick — before the law shows up!

BIG BROTHER *IS* WATCHING

Imagine this.

You're on vacation. Your house is empty. It's four in the morning.

A stranger, dressed all in black, carrying a crowbar, glides up your driveway and around the back of your home. He stops by your back door.

A light flicks on.

"Good evening," a voice says. "Welcome to the Smith home. Say, those are nice pants. Dockers? I didn't know they came in black. Are you looking for anyone in particular? And why do you have that crowbar in your hand?"

The guy is gone halfway through the above speech.

This is real-time monitoring.

Video cameras beam a signal back to a remote location. There's a two-way audio feed, too. The security personnel watching your home can speak through microphones installed at designated locations.

You pick when your home or apartment should be watched. You have the ability to override the system at any time.

Real-time security devices (RTSDs) are in our future. They'll be used at the workplace and in the marketplace. Imagine one at every ATM in the United States. A motion sensor activates the system, and a friendly eye two thousand miles away sees you —

and speaks.

"Welcome to Big Bank. This is Tina with security. Have a good night!" Tina watches you complete your transaction safely, then switches over to an outside camera and watches as you safely get in your car and drive off.

The biggest deterrent to any potential threat against you, your privacy, or your assets is detection. Not after-the-fact detection, but real-time detection — while it's happening.

❑ ❑ ❑ ❑ ❑

If you're ever in a situation where you think you need to have your home/office swept for bugs, i.e., electronic listening devices — don't. Not only are such sweeps fallible, but they also give you a dangerous false sense of security.

A good sweep utilizes sophisticated equipment to detect slight "electronic" irregularities. Pulses and sound waves that can't be attributed to devices such as incandescent lights, answering machines, or telephone systems are then checked further. Sometimes you find a listening device.

Sometimes you don't.

That doesn't mean it's not there.

If the device is not giving off a pulse — if the battery has run out, or if it's been temporarily switched off — guess what? You won't detect it.

Here's a good one:

After months of legal maneuvering out in Ohio, we were finally able to persuade a judge to authorize a legal wiretap on our target individual. It took a four-man crew seven hours to install the devices late one night.

The following day, we settled into a warehouse across the street and began monitoring our target's calls.

The very first conversation we heard was his telling one of his cohorts that he had just called in "professionals" to sweep his telephone lines.

I wanted to call him back and thank him for the advance notice.

We turned off the system so it couldn't be detected.

That took all of five minutes.

The monitoring devices were turned back on the night after our target dropped $2,500 checking for bugs.

Most sensitive information can be reduced to writing and read by the intended viewer in your presence. The document should read "FOR YOUR EYES ONLY" and should be handed back to you. If information is so sensitive then extraordinary measures should be taken, then move the conversation off-site, to a random, never-before-visited location.

❑ ❑ ❑ ❑ ❑

The lesson is quite clear. No matter how apparently great the technology is, it is no better than man and his collective shortcomings.

The human mind still rules. Use the conveniences that come with technology but remember a determined mind can beat any computer or any device anytime.

PLAY DETECTIVE

Hollywood is calling. Listen up, these guys don't have time to waste. Your assignment is to present a few ideas for the show *Mission Impossible*. The producers like technology-based scams. Here's your mission: Identify how five technological advances you use in your daily life could be used against you in a scam. You might consider the telephone, the fax machine, the answering machine, the automobile, the airplane, cell phones, computer banking, a beeper, the tape recorder, the Internet, etc. Next, develop the backup plan you could use to thwart the scam. The MI Force doesn't succeed against you this time!

Here's an example:

Technological advance: **the telephone.** Someone has previously and secretly recorded a loved one's voice. Later, at an appropriate time, the recorded voice is played back to you over the telephone with sufficient background noise to create a little confusion, and at a time when your loved one is known not to be home (perhaps during morning or evening commuting hours). Then a consoling voice gets on the line and explains that your loved one is upset and can't talk, is maybe even hurt. That person, posing as a lawyer, explains that your loved one was involved in a small accident and he fled the scene. He could be charged with a hit-and-run. Before the police get involved, a sum of money can make the people whose car was damaged go away — no insurance, no police — "If we act quickly," he says.

What would your backup plan include?

The scenarios you develop should frighten you, because the scam you come up with could be used by a con man, with just a little luck, against absolutely anyone. The telephone scam above was pulled recently, and successfully, on an intelligent, college-educated woman in the suburbs of Atlanta.

Your goal in thinking of possible scams is to get you prepared and to keep you inquisitive and aware.

You might even give some Hollywood writers some good ideas!

PROTECT YOURSELF

1. **Don't put too much trust in technology.** Even the most advanced systems are designed and administered by people. Remind yourself of problems you've had with technological advances. Have a contingency plan.

2. **If you have an alarm system, test it regularly.** Make sure its integrity hasn't been compromised at any point. The best way to test any alarm system is to activate it. Test each component of the system: the doors, windows, etc.

3. Have a home and office security analysis performed. Have at least two private security firms provide you with a free written estimate. Then call and have the local police walk around your home and office. Ask questions: "What are my available security options? Where do you think a burglar is most likely to enter my home/business?"

4. Don't overlook inexpensive, simple, and effective deterrents. Electrical timers are still a very effective way of making it appear that someone might be home. Use numerous timers and connect at least one timer to a device that makes noise, like a radio. Timers should duplicate your normal level of noise and illumination.

5. Never underestimate human creativity and determination. For good. And for bad. Be prepared for both.

CONCLUSION

LOOKING AHEAD

*"The fantastic advances in the field of electronic communication
constitute a great danger to the privacy of the individual."*
— Supreme Court Chief Justice Earl Warren, 1964

At this very moment . . .

Over twenty-five hundred video cameras are trained on the good citizens of New York City — by their government.

Neighborhood groups in Southern California are hiring investigators to look into the backgrounds of potential neighbors.

The National Security Agency-operated Echelon — a worldwide electronic communications net — is monitoring your phone, E-mail, Internet, fax, and modem-based activity. Indeed, every communication beyond your thoughts is being monitored and analyzed for certain suspicious keywords, accents, and dialects in an effort to thwart terrorist activities. The ability to review the voluminous quantity, and to appropriately and quickly respond, are the only hurdles not yet conquered. Witness the fact that the government had the full information on the World Trade Center bombing six months before it happened. Horribly, the sheer volume of Echelon data prohibited its review before the actual event took place.

Congress is considering a law requiring bankers to determine their customers' normal patterns of transactions. Any deviations would be reported to the government.

A popular department store wants to add medical data to its "Advantage" card, which already contains information about your shopping patterns.

An Internet Web site patent was issued in October 1998 that tracks how many times you actually look at a page that has already been downloaded into your computer.

And some women are walking around with the latest in breast implants — implants containing a numbered microchip, which will allow their "owner" to be identified to the medical profession in case emergency medical treatment is needed. Naturally, this information is not only available to surgeons and hospitals, but it's also available to medical marketers and product manufacturers.

The future is here.

Truly, only your thoughts are your own.

It's appropriate that we've been talking about technology in the last few chapters, because the evolution of the investigative business is inextricably linked with the kind of developments outlined above.

The spycams are going to get smaller. The surveillance equipment will get better. And your personal data is going to continue to spread to computer networks across the land.

It is no longer right to say, "Your secrets are *going to* become everybody's business . . . unless somebody does something." It's too late. Your secrets are already everybody's business and there's really nothing anyone can do about it. You can't put the genie back in the bottle. You can't un-see something.

Join with me in proposing stronger constitutional protection for the American family's privacy than that found in Article 4 of the Bill of Rights ("The right of the people to be secure in their persons, houses, papers, and effects, against unreasonable searches and seizures . . ."). Whether we like it or not, everything we do and communicate is being observed and monitored. The only true safeguard lies in our monitoring the monitoring. Notice and choice are the sole practical options. We should be given notice that we are being reviewed or monitored, when it is occurring, and who is conducting it. And we should be given the choice, if possible, whether to allow the review, or, at least, the choice to challenge or monitor those who are monitoring.

Yes, you're going to be monitored by that camera at the ATM. Yes, your purchases will be analyzed by marketers. And yes, the government is going to do whatever it wants in the interest of national security. That can't be stopped. But you have the right, if nothing else, to be made aware and to appropriately respond.

I believe Jefferson, Washington, Adams, Hamilton, Franklin, and Madison would approve.

As would — of course — the Mustard Man.

A GENTLE REMINDER

Remember what Grandma used to say when your mind wandered during one of her lectures?

What your Uncle Leo said when you told him about some fantastic new scientific advance?

The advice your high-school guidance counselor gave you when confronting a difficult choice?

I'll give you a minute. . . .

With this book, I've attempted to both entertain and inform, to show you, through examples from my experience, the many dangers that come from living in the information age. I hope I have succeeded. You're now more aware of potential unscrupulous attacks and of how you and your family should react to them. Go back over the tips in the book, focusing on ones that particularly ring true to you. Rehearse your defenses.

None of those defenses, however, are as important as what I am about to tell you.

Ready for the answers to those questions now? In reverse order:

Listen to your heart.

Don't believe everything you read/hear/see.

Pay attention.

That's the advice I want to leave you with.

The people who raised you had it right. It's a dangerous world out there. Those who want what you have are constantly bettering their tricks. You have to better your defenses, too.

So trust your intuition. If it looks like a banana, but smells like a lemon, back off.

If something seems too good to be true, it probably is.

And always, above all — pay attention. Help those around you to pay attention, too. And be sure to use your clout as a consumer.

As scary as it is sometimes, we're all in this together.

RESOURCES

The best place to find current information on the state of your privacy rights is the Internet. There's a site relating to virtually every privacy issue. Unfortunately, Internet addresses can change overnight. Use the following addresses as starting points. Remember, it's not called the Web for nothing: Each of the sites mentioned below is connected to many others. Chances are you'll be able to find what you're looking for (and more) by just clicking around. If you have trouble with these addresses, search for the organizations themselves using an Internet search engine, such as **www.dogpile.com**.

A good place to start is **www.privacyrights.org**. This is the home page for the Privacy Rights Clearinghouse. For an interesting take on privacy issues, try the Fight The Fingerprint Web site at **www.networkusa.org/fingerprint.shtml**. The ACLU Web site (**www.aclu.org**) and the Web site for Human Rights USA (**134.84.205.236/whatis.htm**) have links to a number of privacy-issues Web pages.

If you want to do a little digging on current government regulations concerning privacy, you can start at your state's official home page. Every state's official Web address is in the form: **www.state.ny.us** for New York (NY), **www.state.ct.us** for Connecticut (CT), etc. Federal government agencies maintain Web presences as well: Begin with **www.nttc.edu/gov_res.html**. Check out **www.accessreports.com** for instructions on how to access those government documents.

To explore the current state of affairs regarding Internet privacy issues, try **www.eff.org** — the Electronic Frontier Foundation. To find out about remailers and other technological tricks that mask your on-line identity, check out **www.cs.berkeley.edu/~raph/remailer-list.html**. For help in cutting down on junk calls and junk mail, go to:

www.privatecitizen.com

Again, these are only starting points.

BIBLIOGRAPHY

Armstrong, Douglas. "What To Do When Someone Steals Your Identity." *Milwaukee Journal-Sentinel*, February 18, 1999.

Auerbach, Jon G., Mark Maremont, and Gary Putka. "Prying Eyes." *The Wall Street Journal*, November 5, 1998.

Bachrach, Judy. "Clinton's Private Eye." *Vanity Fair*, September 1998.

Boal, Mark. "Spy Cam Chic." *Village Voice*, December 8, 1998.

Boal, Mark. "Surveillance City." *Village Voice*, October 6, 1998.

Bray, Hiawatha. "Privacy Advocates Decry Digital Fingerprints." *Boston Globe*, March 9, 1999.

"DNA Testing Proposals." *New York Times*, December 17, 1998.

Ellis, John. "The Real Dollars are in Databases." *Boston Globe*, February 25, 1999.

"The Eyes Have It." *Continental In-Flight Magazine*, March 1999.

Feldman, Gayle. "Direct from Scanner to Printed Page." *New York Times*, July 27, 1998.

Frantz, Douglas. "Chiquita Still Under Cloud After Newspaper's Retreat." *New York Times*, July 17, 1998.

Gerrard, Mike. "On-Line Detective on the Case." *Guardian*, August 13, 1992.

Givens, Beth and the Privacy Rights Clearinghouse. *The Privacy Rights Handbook*. Avon: New York, 1997.

Goldberg, Matt. "I Spy." *The Village Voice*, November 10, 1998.

Guart, Al. "Feds: Nigerian Rings Slickest Yet." *New York Post*, January 3, 1999.

Hafner, Katie. "Chiquita Case Illustrates Vulnerability of Voice Mail." *New York Times*, July 23, 1998.

Harmon, Amy. "E-Mail Takes the Stand and Companies Take a Stand on E-Mail." *New York Times*, November 11, 1998.

"High-Tech Snooping Targets Employees' E-Mail." Associated Press, March 6, 1999.

Hoffmann, Bill. "Feds: Fotog Tapped into Tom-Nicole Spat." *New York Post*, December 11, 1998.

Kelley, Tina. "Security Fears Still Plague Cybershopping." *New York Times*, July 30, 1998.

Lange, Larry. "Biometry: Human-Tracking System Goes Global." *Electronic Engineering Times*, February 3, 1997.

Long, Robert Emmet, ed. *Rights To Privacy*. H.W. Wilson: New York, 1997.

Love, Douglas. "Speed, Rage, and Videotape." *Car & Travel*, February 1999.

Markoff, John. "Growing Compatibility Issue: Computers and User Privacy." *New York Times*, March 3, 1999.

Markoff, John. "Microsoft to Alter Software in Response to Privacy Concerns." *New York Times*, March 7, 1999.

McAllester, Matthew. "Identity Crisis." *Newsday*, September 30, 1998.

McKinley, James Jr. "U.S. Agents Raid Stores in 24 Cities to Seize Spy Gear." *New York Times*, April 6, 1995.

O'Harrow, Robert Jr. "Posting a Privacy Problem?" *Washington Post*, January 22, 1999.

O'Harrow, Robert Jr., and Liz Leyden. "U.S. Helped Fund License Photo Database." *Washington Post*, February 18, 1999.

Packard, Vance. *The Naked Society*. Van Rees: New York, 1964.

Pear, Robert. "Not for Identification Purposes (Just Kidding)." *New York Times*, October 4, 1998.

"Privacy Groups Urge Boycott of Intel." Associated Press, January 25, 1999.

"Questions for Edmund J. Pankau." *New York Times Magazine*, January 17, 1999.

Quittner, Joshua. "Going Private." *Time*, February 5, 1999.

Ramp, Stefanie. "Confessions of a Credit Card Thief." *Westchester County Weekly*, December 17, 1998.

"Raytheon Suit Raises Web Privacy Issues." Associated Press, March 15, 1999.

Rivais, Larry. "They're After Your Information." *Springfield Union-News*, February 22, 1999.

Rothfeder, Jeffrey. *Privacy for Sale*. Simon and Schuster: New York, 1992.

"Scams, Stings and Con Games." *City of New York*, May 1998.

"Shadowing Teens." *Car & Travel*, February 1999.

Stapleton, Jay. "Face Lift." *Our Town*, September 1, 1998.

Stolberg, Sheryl Gay. "Medical I.D.'s and Privacy (or What's Left of It)." *New York Times*, October 11, 1998.

Tharp, Paul. "SEC: 'World's Oldest Con Man' Even Duped Former U.N. Diplomat." *New York Post*, April 4, 1995.

"Top Pathologist Joins Defense Lineup." *USA Today*, June 30, 1994.

"Vacations from Hell." *Consumer Reports*, January 1999.

Vest, Jason. "Shhh, They're Listening." *The Village Voice*, August 18, 1998.

Weld, Eric Sean. "Never-Ending Nightmare." *Hampshire Life*, January 29, 1999.

Wells, Susan J. "No, Not That John Gotti." *New York Times*, October 22, 1998.

Younger, Joseph D. "Thwarting Car Thieves, One at a Time." *Car & Travel*, February 1999.

In Chapter 3, Justice Brennan is quoted from his dissent in CALIFORNIA v. GREENWOOD ET AL., No. 86-684, SUPREME COURT OF THE UNITED STATES. 486 U.S. 35; 108 S. Ct. 1625; 1988 U.S. LEXIS 2279; 100 L. Ed. 2d 30; 56. U.S.L.W. 4409. January 11, 1988, Argued; May 16, 1988, Decided.

Information about the U.S. Postal Inspectors was gleaned from their Web site at **www.usps.gov/postalinspectors/faq-is.html**.